Confident Parenting In a Complex World

by
Janice Gabe

Published by:
Professional Resource Publications
P.O. Box 501485
Indianapolis, IN 46256

© Copyright 2011 Janice Gabe. All rights reserved. No part of this book may be reproduced by any means without the expressed written consent of the author.

Library of Congress Cataloging - in Publication Data

Confident Parenting in a Complex World by Janice Gabe
Front cover illustrated by Allan Miller.
Graphics and layout designed by Rexene Lane.

ISBN: 0-963 9023-6-8 (pbk. :alk)

First Edition

Parenting-nonfiction

Manufactured in the United States of America

To dedicated moms and dads everywhere
who have the courage to parent their children
and
all the incredible young people that I have
been blessed to know over the years.

Acknowledgments

There are several important people that I would like to acknowledge and thank.

My two favorite parents, Sharon Grimes and Fran Gabe;

My husband and parenting partner, Steve Gabe;

My two amazing sons, Kyle and Chris, who have been a source of joy, pride and inspiration;

My wonderful assistant, Barb Osborne; I would not do what I do, if she was not so incredible at what she does.

Contents

Introduction   x

Chapter One
Value Based Parenting   1

Being a Value Centered Parent
Identifying Core Family Values
Family Rules Tie Back to Core Values
Role Modeling Family Values
Establishing a Value Based Support Network
Media Impact on Values
Sharing Our Value Heritage
Family Plan for Value Development

Chapter Two
Value Based Consequences   21

Giving Value Based Consequences
Taking Responsibility

Components of Effective Consequences
Consequences Teach Values
Atonement Based Consequences
Restitution Based Consequences
Restitution Based Category Guidelines
Selecting the Correct Category
Consequences Over a Period of Time
Deliver Consequences with Empathy
Consequences of Attachment
Life is a Good Teacher
Assume the Best
Beyond the Home
Timing is Everything
An Emotional, Behavioral or Learning Diagnosis

Chapter Three
Dealing with Dishonesty 61

Dishonesty in Children and Teens
Lying to Solve or Avoid Problems
Inventing Tales and Exaggerating
Habitual and Pathological Lying

Chapter Four
The Technologically Savvy Parent 71

The Most Recent Parenting Challenge
Screen Time and Development

Cognitive Development
Social Development
Empathy Development
Having a Plan
When Screens Should be Introduced
Facebook and Social Networking Sites
If Technology Becomes an Obsession
Unplug and Tune In

Chapter Five
Confidence, Wit & Wisdom   95

Parenting with Confidence, Wit and Wisdom
Long Term Commitments with Long Term Payoffs

About the author...   105

Make an order   107

Introduction

As a child, adolescent and family therapist, I spend a great deal of time each week talking with parents who are concerned about doing the best job of parenting their children as they possibly can. Parents struggle to maintain their confidence as they are faced with the realization that the world is changing quickly, becoming increasingly complex, and presenting parents with challenges that previous generations of parents could not have imagined.

The cultures in our schools, communities and families are ever changing. However, some things have not changed. Parents of this generation are concerned about possessing the skills and confidence to teach their children a value system that will help them grow up to be happy, productive, competent and contributing members of our culture. Parents are concerned about how to discipline their children effectively and confidently. Perhaps most importantly, parents are concerned about how to confidently parent with the constantly changing culture of technology.

Value based parenting is a tough job. Utilizing discipline in an effective manner can be difficult. Understanding and responding to technology can be challenging. The goal of this book is to enhance parental confidence by providing guidelines for developing a family atmosphere that promotes value development, utilizes effective discipline and responds appropriately to technology.

Confident parents respond to their children in a calm, consistent, firm, nurturing and loving manner. They maintain their composure, their sense of humor and their common sense. They listen to their children without feeling they have to give in, or consent to their desires. They treat their children with respect and dignity, and require that their children treat them the same. They allow their children to be true to their basic personalities, without tolerating inappropriate behavior. As a result of reacting to their children with confidence, parents will be rewarded with confidence from their children.

CHAPTER ONE
Value Based Parenting

Being a Value Centered Parent

Parenting presents many challenges and parents often find themselves questioning their decisions and their interaction with their children. Parents often seek the advice of others, only to find they are more confused as others offer them a variety of opinions. These opinions are often contradictory. Clarifying values assists parents in becoming centered. Having a clear understanding of what values you want to pass on to your children provides you with a rudder for your ship so you do not feel like you are casting about in the tumultuous seas of parenting with no direction. Values provide you with an anchor which holds your family securely in place. Values provide you with a compass; they become a way to navigate if you feel your family has gotten off course. They will give you confidence in answering day to day parenting questions such as:

➤ *What advice do I listen to?* (You listen to advice that supports your value system.)

➤ *How do I know what things to let slide and what things to take a stance on?* (You take a stance on things that are a reflection of the values you are trying to teach.)

➤ *Is this the right parenting choice even if no one else seems to have the same rules for their children?* (It is the right choice if it fits with your value system.)

Perhaps most importantly, values become a unifying force between parents. In most families there is one individual in the relationship who is a bit stricter and perhaps a bit more rigid in interpreting the rules. This is typically balanced by another individual in the relationship who is less strict and more flexible. This combination works well until children are introduced into the equation. The strict parent often finds themselves being stricter in response to the parent whom they feel "lets the kids get away with too much." The more lenient parent responds by being even more lenient to compensate for the stricter parent. Soon, instead of responding to the child's behavior, parents are responding to their partner's response to the child's behavior. As a result, parents are becoming increasingly more frustrated with one another and each parent feels isolated in their parenting.

The reality is, children can survive and thrive with parents who each bring a different perspective to their parenting. However, they cannot survive parents who are worlds apart in their parenting. In reality, most parents are not worlds apart from each other, until they stop reacting to the child, and start reacting to the other parent's reaction to the child. The best way to reunify is to give some thought to it, and come to some agreement about what values parents want to teach their children. This allows parents to focus on their similarities instead of their differences. The parents might have different methods for teaching these values and that is okay. If parents can agree upon values, the parenting differences are much easier to resolve.

Ultimately, raising children with strong value systems will equip your children with tools for excellent decision making, with confidence in and commitment to their belief systems, and the skills they need to be happy and competent in their world.

Identifying Core Family Values

This generation of parents needs to take an aggressive approach in promoting their values. Organizational psychologists long ago identified that any strong

-Value Based Parenting

corporation has at its core a set of values which provide the corporation with focus and direction. The goals, objectives and structure of a corporation are all avenues by which their values become "operationalized." Families are no different. In order for families to run effectively, there must be a core value system which holds the family together and gives it meaning, purpose, strength and direction. The core values need to be established by the heads of the house, just as corporate values are established by the heads of the organization.

Identifying core family values is an important task that requires a great deal of reflection and thought. I often ask parents to work together to identify what they consider to be the five most important values in their family. These five core values serve as the guiding force for the family and provide a base for how the family operates. Once parents have established these values, they need to write them down in a place where they are visible to all members of the family. The five core values will serve as the basis for how the parents treat one another, how they treat their children, how the children treat one another, and how the family interacts with the world.

Family values are statements that are written in a positive manner (what we believe in, not what we can or cannot do), and are broad enough to encompass a wide range of behavior. It is important to remember that there are no "correct" family values. Each family has to establish these for themselves. However, the following are examples of core family values:

➤ *We are a family that listens to each other.*

➤ *In this family, everyone takes responsibility for*

(their behavior, their feelings, and their things).

➤ *Everyone matters and counts and will be treated accordingly.*

➤ *Everyone has something important to offer.*

➤ *Honor and trust make our family work.*

➤ *We need contributions from each person in order for our family to work.*

➤ *Setting goals and working for our goals is how we find happiness and develop self esteem.*

➤ *We celebrate our blessings by sharing with others.*

My oldest son is used to hearing us talk about our family values. When he was young, and we would interrupt him before he had completed his thought, he quickly reminded us, "But we are a family that listens and I'm not done talking!" Of course over and over he has put this value to the test, since we have been blessed with a child who is extremely verbal.

When my oldest son was young and would hear something often, he assumed that it was a part of our family values system. Something that he heard often was, "You can't have everything you see on TV." My son once asked if he could have a brother or sister, and I informed him that he could not. He stated, "MOM, I think I should be able to have it because it's not something I saw on TV!"

Family Rules Tie Back to Core Values

Life does not come with a rule book which governs

behavior. Ultimately, children need to learn to make decisions about their behavior, not based on rules, but on values. Therefore, the rules and expectations which are established in the home, work best when they relate back to the core values. This teaches children not only how to behave, but why certain behavior is appropriate and why certain behavior is not. When discussing behavior with children, attaching value based meaning to behavior is important. When kids ask, "Why can't we do that?" parents can take this opportunity to teach children that certain behavior is not acceptable because that behavior is inconsistent with the family's values. Similarly, when we ask children to do things, we have an opportunity to teach value development. When we ask children to put their toys away, we can tell them that in this family everyone is responsible, and that part of being responsible is taking care of your things by putting them away. When we talk to our children about telling us the truth, we can remind them that honor and trust are things that make our family work. This value base will help guide children in their decision making process as they grow and mature.

Role Modeling Family Values

When identifying core family values, it is important to select values that you are willing to role model for your children. Often, parents select behaviors to reinforce and promote in their children that the parents wish they had themselves. For example, parents might view themselves as not being assertive enough and they might feel this lack of assertion has created problems for them throughout their lives. As a result, they may place a great deal of importance on assertiveness in their children because they want to protect their children from experiencing the same types of problems which they have encountered. The parents might identify a value, "In this family, everyone speaks their mind and sticks up for themselves." However, if parents cannot role model these values, they will appear hypocritical to the children. Therefore, parents must have a commitment to the values they select and must behave in such a manner that this commitment is evident to the children. Nothing sabotages value development as much as parents behaving in a way that is inconsistent with the values which they tell their children they hold important.

It is important to remember that adults teach children by action as well as words. One way to model behavior and values is to explain adult behavior by discussing the values that are driving this behavior. Parents have many opportunities to teach in this fashion. For example, parents may choose to explain to their children how they themselves are dealing with anger. If the parents become angry with a child and feel that they may say something that they will regret to the child, it is healthy for the parent to explain that they are not going to discuss this with the child right now, because they (the parents) are angry and might not be able to discuss the issue in a respectful fashion. Parents send powerful value based messages to their children when they are able to say, "I am angry now and when I am angry, I may say things that I do not mean. I don't like what comes out of my mouth when I am angry and I don't like feeling out of control. So, I am going to wait until I cool down before we talk about this." The values that come out in this message are clear. Parents are telling their children, "I am responsible for my feelings, I am responsible for how I deal with these feelings, and I believe in respecting others, no matter how strong my feelings may be right now."

Sometimes the most effective way to promote value based behavior with our children is to explain our value based decisions. If we want our children to watch less TV, we need

-Value Based Parenting

to turn off the TV, and announce that the family has wasted too much valuable time in front of the television and it is time to change that behavior. If parents want children to go to church, parents can explain why they enjoy going to church. If parents want children to value honesty, parents can let the waitress know she under billed them and explain to children that they can enjoy their meal more knowing that they behaved in an honorable fashion.

Modeling through explanation is a particularly helpful teaching strategy for children with impulsive disorders and Attention Deficit Hyperactivity Disorders. Research suggests that these children tend to get in trouble because they have poorly developed internal self speech. Self speech is the primary mechanism by which people control their impulses. In effect, sharing the internal self speech that goes into making value based choices teaches children how to better develop their own internal speech.

I once had an ADHD young man tell me, "I just need to learn to stop and think." What the young man was telling me was that he needed to activate his internal self speech. When I asked him what he needed to think about, he replied, "I don't know. No one has ever told me." In other words, "I don't know how to activate my internal self speech." When adults openly discuss how they come to conclusions about decisions, it helps children develop this skill.

A Value Based Support Network

Once parents have established their core values, it is important that they develop a network of friends and relatives that share similar values. My parents had seven children, and they had a lot of help raising their children. Parents cannot teach values in isolation. When I was growing up, my parents set forth a value system that was reinforced by my extended family, at school, at church, by my neighbors, in activities in which I participated, and by my friends' parents. These networks are important in reinforcing values, and they are not always readily available to children in our current culture. Therefore, one of the most important things parents can do for themselves and their children is to establish a network that will help them in reinforcing the value messages they are striving to teach.

Parents need to take time to ask themselves, "Who are the people and institutions in my life that will provide another layer of value development and help me in reinforcing the values I am trying to teach my children?" If parents do not have a network, several things happen. First of all, they are not receiving any support or reinforcement for how they are trying to raise their children. Without this support, parents become exhausted and begin to question their competence. When parents question their competence, it makes it difficult for them to remain strong and confident in their value based decisions. If parents do not have a network, they become vulnerable to peer pressure exerted from their children's friends.

I once had a group of sixth graders tell me that if they wanted to do something that they knew their parents would not approve of, they would begin "working" the parents. The entire group would go to one house and badger the parents into giving their child permission. They would begin with the parent whom they felt was the easiest to convince and move forward from there. They would all tell that parent that the other moms and dads had already given permission and that they were the last hold out. The first parent would cave in, and the group would move on to its next victim, and even though most of the parents were uncomfortable with the request, they would cave because they believed other

-Value Based Parenting

parents were caving. The group of boys would complain that there was one parent in particular that would foil their plans. Because she was difficult, they would approach her last, and hit her with "everyone else has already said its okay." I laughed out loud as the boys told me that this mom would confidently respond, "Well, I don't care if God lets Jesus do it, my son will not be participating!" The problem is that there is a tremendous amount of power in networking. If the kids are networking, (and believe me, they do) and the parents are not, then the kids are the ones who end up with the power.

Parents need to feel comfortable with the fact that the values they are trying to promote are being reinforced by others in the child's life. Family friends, baby-sitters, school, church and relationships with extended family members need chosen with this in mind. When I have parents who ask me what else they can do to be better value based parents, I often tell them that they do not need to parent more, they need to network more.

Media Impact on Values

Parents have a responsibility to monitor the value messages their children are exposed to in the media. Research clearly indicates that the media influences behavior in children. Recent research suggests witnessing violent media actually alters the brain in a manner very similar to the way the brain is altered when children are victims of violence. Young adolescents who watch R-rated movies are more likely to use profane language, smoke, drink and experiment with sexual behavior. Violent media increases violent behavior in many children.

Parents sometimes make the mistake of comparing the

Confident Parenting In A Complex World-

media they were exposed to as children, to the media their children are exposed to currently. The media of today is different than the media of past decades. Children are exposed to more media, at an earlier age, with less parental supervision. Prime time television programming is often adult themed and highly inappropriate for children. Media in this decade includes not only music and television, but videos that kids watch over and over until they have memorized each scene. Music videos add a visual component to music, thereby increasing its impact.

Online computer systems and video games are an important source of media exposure. Parents who have school age children playing video games need to pay close attention to the context and themes of these games. The graphics on the screen are highly realistic, and portray extensive people to people violence. This understandably has a significant impact on children who spend endless hours in front of the screen. This video culture is very different than exposure to Pac Man. (A rather benign game in which a little ball ate dots as it made its way across the screen.) Not only are the games themselves violent, they take on a dimension of realism because games are so interactive as individuals play and communicate with others online. The lines between virtual and real blur more as children and teens play games in which they create characters. Children and teens complain that they are being mistreated or "bullied" by fellow gamers on service sights.

As the lines become more blurred, the stronger the impact the games will have on value development. This issue will be addressed in more detail in Chapter 4.

The media provides ghastly details into the personal lives and behaviors of famous people. Over exposure to such media normalizes that behavior in the minds of children.

-Value Based Parenting

This behavior is often inconsistent with the behavior parents are trying to teach their children. When current events, political events and the behavior of famous people are inconsistent with the values parents are trying to teach their children, parents need to openly discuss this discrepancy with their children.

Similarly, parents need to take a strong stand on the value messages presented in video games, television, movies and music. Much of the media that children are exposed to relays two powerful messages:

➤ *Violence is the first course of conflict resolution.*

➤ *Good guys and bad guys solve problems the same way, through violence. The only difference is that violence is okay when you are in the right.*

This creates significant problems since most children always believe that they are in the right.

In order to combat the negative influences of media, parents can select movies and books that reinforce children with positive value messages. In addition, parents can tell their children stories from childhood which helped shape their values. Children love to hear stories about their parents as children. Many adults can remember significant events which happened to them that shaped their beliefs about the world, about people, and about what is right and wrong.

Since we know that media does impact children and influence their behavior, it is wise to ask ourselves how we can use media to get our message across. I have a good friend who was quite appalled by some of her ten year old son's movie requests. She reviewed a list of some of her favorite movies and evaluated the value messages in them.

It then became her summer project to expose her son to these movies. Many of these movies were old, so her son had not heard of them. Her son loved the movies. They shared time together watching and discussing them. He became so intrigued by these old movies that he soon forgot about his own list.

With the increasing popularity of iPods, portable DVD players and internet access via cell phones, it has become a challenge for parents to monitor what their children are listening to today. We know that music is a powerful source of socialization for children. Parents should not hesitate to censor and restrict what their children are exposed to through any media. When selecting music, books or movies for the family, keep in mind to make choices that reinforce your values.

Sharing Our Value Heritage

We did not learn our values in isolation. We learned them from a rich source of adults, institutions, extended family, and neighborhoods. Most adults can identify particular events that occurred in their life which drove a powerful value home for them.

I remember as a child in second grade there was a girl who the other kids did not like. She was often the object of ridicule and rejection. I told my mother that I did not want to send her a valentine. My mother did not scold me or lecture me, but she did tell me a story about her childhood

She told me that there was a similar girl in her class at school. My mother was always nice to her because she felt bad that she was so mistreated. My mother gave in to peer pressure and decided not to send her a valentine. She was the only classmate being excluded. My mother arrived at school to discover that this child had purchased a special Valentine's Day gift for her. She was overcome with guilt and spent her morning crafting a handmade valentine for this child. The child responded by being very grateful that my mother had taken the time to make her a special valentine, one that stood out from the rest.

My mother proceeded to tell me that at that moment, she learned that being kind to people was more important than being part of the crowd. She left me to think about her story. That is the moment that I remember internalizing the value that people matter, and count, and should be treated accordingly. I, in turn, shared this story with my son. I also shared the many stories of my childhood that make up my value heritage. Not only did he respond, he has often begged me to tell him these stories over and over. It is my hope that the messages stay with him forever and he passes them on to his children.

Nothing we do as parents is any more important than value development. Values provide guidance, direction, focus and a sense of self awareness for children. These are things that they will carry with them for the rest of their lives. Values are our legacy and our gifts to our children.

The following pages will provide the reader with an opportunity to reflect on the material presented in this chapter and develop a plan for implementing value development.

Confident Parenting In A Complex World-

Family Plan for Value Development

A. What are the five most important values for our family?

1. _____
_____
_____

2. _____
_____
_____

3. _____
_____
_____

4. _____
_____
_____

5. _____
_____
_____

B. Where can we post these values so they will be visible to all members of our family?
_____
_____

-Value Based Parenting

_____
_____

C. How can we build our value network?

1. Who are the people in our lives that support our family values? How can we promote our relationships with these people?

_____
_____
_____
_____
_____
_____
_____

2. What are the values based activities in which my children participate?

_____
_____
_____
_____

3. What are the values based activities in which I would like our family to become more involved?

_____
_____
_____
_____

Confident Parenting In A Complex World-

D. What are our rules and how are they connected to our family values?

_____
_____
_____
_____
_____
_____
_____
_____
_____

E. What did my behavior today teach my children about values?

_____
_____
_____
_____
_____

F. What type of media messages are my children receiving?

1. What do my children watch on television? What are the value messages they are being exposed to on TV?

How many hours do my children spend watching TV, movies and videos?

_____
_____

What are my children's five favorite TV shows?

_____
_____

-Value Based Parenting

What are my children's favorite musical groups?

2. What video games do my children play and what are the value messages they portray?

3. What are some values based books, stories, or movies that I would like my children exposed to?

G. What are the most vivid memories I have as a child about my value development? How have I shared these with my children?

Confident Parenting In A Complex World-

CHAPTER TWO

Value Based Consequences

Giving Value Based Consequences

As parents, we are concerned about learning new and effective techniques for dealing with problematic behaviors of our children. We search for the best way, the right way, the proper way to parent our children. We are in search of the absolute right answers regarding spanking, time-outs, grounding and consequences. In order to provide effective parenting, we must look beyond techniques and absolutes. We must remember that the primary role of parents is to provide discipline that not only addresses behavior, but teaches values and encourages moral development. Techniques alone cannot accomplish this task. We have to look beyond the immediate and keep in mind the long-term goals of parenting.

Parents often want professionals to tell them what they should do in every situation. This is not something that can be accomplished, and it is not something that is necessary. In the pages that follow, we are going to focus on the use of consequences as a discipline for children and teens. I cannot write a book that gives a consequence for every possible situation. Such a book is not necessary. I can, however, lay forth guidelines for effective value based consequences. Effective use of consequences in parenting addresses behavior, teaches value lessons, and strengthens character These are, after all, the goals of parenting.

Taking Responsibility

Consequences allow children the respect and dignity to take responsibility for themselves and for their behavior. When we interfere with children experiencing consequences of their behavior, we rob them of valuable learning experiences, we delay their maturation, and we do them a disservice by preventing them from being prepared to meet the demands of the adult world. Parents protect their children from consequences because they love their children, want to protect them from frustration and failure, and want them to have pleasant, rewarding childhoods. Parents do not want to suffer the pain of watching their children struggle with the learning process.

We forget that allowing children to experience small, controlled failures while they are young can prevent them from experiencing huge and devastating failures as adults. Effective consequences place responsibility for the child's behavior back on the child, where the responsibility belongs. Parents spend a great deal of time and energy warning children of possible consequences, threatening, lecturing and then rescuing. Thus, the parents are taking responsibility for their children, and then end up becoming frustrated because the children never seem to learn.

By allowing children to take responsibility for their own behavior, we are also teaching the value of responsibility. This is a value that cannot be taught by lecturing, explaining, discussing or warning. Learning the value of responsibility requires the active participation of the child. Without this value, children will not be prepared to move into adulthood.

The following is an example of parents who allowed consequences to be a good teacher.

My neighbor, Chris, has a wonderful daughter. When her daughter was eleven years old, Chris and her family were excited about a family vacation to the beach. Chris had spent a great deal of time helping her family pack for the trip. Chris's daughter was responsible for packing her own bags, a task which she was perfectly capable of completing. Chris encouraged her daughter to give her bags a second

-Value Based Consequences

look to make sure she had not forgotten to pack something essential, but her daughter did not want to take the time to do this boring task.

When they arrived at their destination, her daughter discovered she had forgotten to pack her swimsuit. Chris did not rant, lecture or get angry. She calmly informed her daughter that they would not be purchasing her another suit. Her daughter was initially shocked by her mother's response. When she realized that her mother was serious, she resigned herself to the fact that she would spend the week swimming in a T-shirt and shorts.

Chris admitted that it was difficult for her to see her daughter suffer, but she knew that learning responsibility was more important than her daughter being properly attired at the beach. Her daughter has packed for many vacations since that time, and she has done so without leaving a single essential item out.

As our culture becomes more and more consumeristic, we find it easy to overindulge children materialistically. Upon hearing the above story, many parents comment that under the same circumstances, they would purchase a new swimming suit, because they could "well afford it." Being able to afford a new swimming suit is not the issue. Being willing to teach our children responsibility, is the issue.

We have become a parenting culture that excuses our children's inappropriate behavior by blaming teachers, ourselves, children's friends, and society for our children's behavior. Because of this, children continue to make poor choices and behave inappropriately. They have no motivation to do things differently. We become angry and defensive when someone discusses our child's inappropriate behavior. We consider that to be a reflection on us.

Therefore, when our child's behavior comes into question, we feel our parenting skills are being called into question. This defensiveness fuels our tendency to excuse our children's behavior, expecting others to do the same. In effect, our ego gets in the way of our children's maturing and learning.

My father had seven children. When one of us behaved inappropriately, he never viewed this as a reflection of his parenting. He viewed it as our behavior, and made it clear that we were expected to handle our behavior. As a result, we grew up to be responsible adults who are competent and capable of taking control of our lives.

Life is a good teacher. Each day is full of learning opportunities for our children. Effective parenting requires that we take advantage of these learning opportunities, not get in the way of them.

Components of Effective Consequences

The following is an example of an effective consequence.

A young adolescent male was referred to my office because he had been caught shoplifting. The parents took this behavior very seriously, and set forth a series of consequences for him. They discovered he had been stealing for quite some time. They asked him to make a list of all the items he had taken. They calculated the value of these items, and had him do work around the house until his debt was completely worked off. He was not allowed to watch TV, play Nintendo, or leave the house until this was completed. One of the chores assigned was to scoop dog poop out of the back yard. When he had worked off the proper amount, his parents informed him that he would go

-Value Based Consequences

to the bank, purchase a money order, and send it to a charity of his choice.

When I talked to the young man about this consequence, he told me that he did not like the consequence, but that he was grateful for it. When I asked him to explain, he said that the consequence was helping him, because he had felt bad about his stealing for a long time. He thought that by completing the consequence, he could put the stealing behavior behind him and not continue to feel so bad about himself. He thought if he did not feel so bad about himself, he would be less likely to steal again. He also shared that whenever he was working on his consequence, it gave him time to think about his behavior. He admitted that he had been tempted to steal again, but when he thought about it, he could smell all that dog poop and decided against it.

This was a very effective consequence because it placed the responsibility for the behavior on the child. It was action oriented and required effort on his part. It occurred over a period of time, requiring him to think about his behavior and the effect it had on others. Perhaps most importantly, the consequence helped him to feel better, because he felt he was able to correct his wrong and feel somehow atoned for his behavior.

Effective value based consequences have the following components:

➤ *They place the responsibility back on the child.*

➤ *They teach values.*

➤ *They are action oriented and require effort on the part of the child.*

➤ They are atonement based.

➤ They are restitution based.

➤ They extend over time, and encourage the child to think about their behavior.

➤ They are delivered with empathy and concern on the part on of the parents.

Consequences Teach Values

Consequences must encourage children to look at the value base that drives their behavior. Without this, the learning process is not complete. Children, between the ages of five and seven, need to become socially aware. Part of this social awareness, is understanding one's self as being part of a community. This means learning that our behaviors have an impact on those around us. In short, it means developing empathy for others and an awareness of others' feelings. Children who learn this are better adjusted socially, are better behaved in school, and are more likely to experience success in all areas of their lives. As children develop empathy, they begin to realize that if certain things make them feel bad, then their actions also may make others feel bad. They begin to realize that they need to adjust their behavior to consider the needs and feelings of others. The primary value that we need to teach younger children is the value of empathy and understanding. Therefore, when disciplining children, it is important to teach them to think about how their behavior impacts others.

Atonement Based Consequences

People often think that in order for consequences to be effective, they must cause children great pain or at least

-Value Based Consequences

significant discomfort. In other words, people often think that consequences should hurt or make the child feel bad about their behavior. One of the roles of discipline is that it allows children to feel better about themselves. Actually, the best consequences allow children to feel better about themselves, upon having completed the consequence. They are able to atone for their behavior, and leave it behind. Atonement based consequences very simply allow children to reflect on their behavior, think about the right and wrong of their behavior, and make amends for it. By doing this they are able to forgive themselves. They also learn the value of righting wrongs and making amends.

Restitution Based Consequences

People often think of restitution based consequences in terms of money. I refer to restitution as the concept of cleaning up one's messes. Consequences that are connected to their behavior make the most sense to children. Restitution based consequences are directly connected to the behavior. The concept of restitution is very simple. If you break it you fix it, if you take something you must give it back, if you do something mean you must do an act of kindness. Restitution is helpful for many reasons. It encourages the development of empathy for others and requires action, effort and thought on the part of the child. It also teaches problem solving skills. If a child has done a behavior that is harmful to another, and he/she is unable to make restitution with that particular person, restitution can be made to the community, neighborhood, or school by participating in volunteer work or community service. If a child is cruel to someone or destroys property, there are many ways they can be held accountable to pay restitution.

A few years ago several grade school boys rode their bikes

Confident Parenting In A Complex World-

through a neighbor's yard on their way to school. In the process, they destroyed the lawn. As they were riding off, the home owner asked them several times to stop. When the boys ignored her request,, she took a very bold but appropriate course of action. She called their parents. The parental responses were varied. Some parents apologized for their children. Some parents became angry at her, telling her she was making a big deal out of nothing. Some parents sent their children over to apologize. One parent restricted their son's use of the bike and gave him a lecture about respect and not being misled by peer pressure. One very creative mother informed her son that he would be required to assist the neighbor with yard work. She further instructed him that he would do the yard work with a courteous attitude and to the best of his ability. When someone asked her what would happen if he refused, the mom calmly replied that his privileges would be suspended until he decided to comply. Her exact statement was, "Life as he knows it, will be over.

Interestingly enough, many of the parents complained that they felt the mom was being too punitive and too harsh on her ten year old child. However, as time went on, that child never rode his bike through another neighbor's lawn again, even though several of the other kids involved in the incident continued to do so. The child who completed the yard work learned about personal responsibility and experienced first hand the consequences of "going along with the crowd." He learned about empathy for others because he developed an appreciation of how much work goes into keeping a lawn nice. He learned many lessons that prepared him for adulthood. Unfortunately, many of the other boys involved in the incident were robbed of a valuable learning experience. It may take many more conflicts with neighbors, teachers, and possibly the police before some of these boys learn these lessons. By intervening early, we can save our children from more painful lessons later on. At age ten, the risks are small. At fifteen the risk becomes greater, and at twenty-two, the risks can become devastating.

Restitution Based Category Guidelines

There are six simple guidelines that assist parents in effectively utilizing restitution based consequences. Most behaviors, that warrant an action-oriented value based consequence, fit into one of six categories. Each of these categories has a physical dimension and a relationship dimension.

Category One: If you abuse it you lose it. If a "take away" consequence seems most appropriate for the situation, then try to follow this guideline. This is, of course, a very simple concept and helps keep the behavior and issues in the forefront of the discipline.

In the physical dimension, children and teens lose things they have used in an irresponsible fashion. If you abuse the phone you lose the phone, if you abuse the car, you lose the car, or if you abuse your toys, you lose the use of those toys. I have, in extreme cases, even recommended to parents that their child loses the use of their room. This recommendation has been made in situations where the child or teen trashed their room, locked themselves in their room, or snuck out of their bedroom window at night. Parents were instructed to purchase locks for the outside of the room, and have the child sleep on the couch for a few days. The child has access to only a few essential items from their room, such as a few changes of clothing. This type of consequence makes a powerful statement to children and seldom has to be used more than once.

In the relationship dimension, if the child abuses trust, they lose trust, and if they abuse their freedom, then they lose freedom.

It is important to keep in mind when children and teens "lose" these things, they lose them for a designated period of time. It is not helpful to tell children things like "I will never be able to trust you again." The adolescent mind basically says, "Hey, if you aren't ever going to trust me, no matter what I do, then I might as well do what I want!"

Category Two: If you want the goodies, you have to be kind to the vendors. That's right folks, we are the vendors. The goodies are ours to dispense as we deem appropriate. Many children feel they live at the end of a one way street where everything comes their way, and they do not have a responsibility to give anything back.

I see many examples of this behavior wherever kids and parents gather. Parents take time out of their schedules to accommodate their children, by taking them to sporting events, shopping trips, birthday parties, and video stores. It amazes me that these children then talk to their parents in hateful tones, order their parents around, criticize them, or throw temper tantrums. Parents respond to this by continuing to take their children wherever they want to go, when they want to go, and buying them whatever they demand.

It appears that parents think they do not have any recourse. When I talk to parents about this, they have a variety of reasons why they tolerate this inappropriate behavior. I hear things like, "I didn't think I should prevent him from going to the birthday party, because I had already RSVP'd." and "I didn't want them to miss practice because we made a

-Value Based Consequences

commitment to the team." or "I really needed to get the back-to-school shopping done."

Children need to understand that their parents are obligated to do certain things for them, such as, provide them with a home, food, clothes and education. However, there are many things that parents do, that are not required of them. It is perfectly acceptable, and sometime necessary, for parents parents to let their children know, "We are happy to do the many extra things for you, and yet we do require that you treat us with respect, or you will not continue to receive these goodies." To continue to give to children when they are not required to give anything in return, does not prepare them for future relationships.

In fact, I have often had children take a piece of paper, and draw a line down the middle. On the right side, I have them record everything their parents have done for them in the past week. On the left side, I ask them to write down everything they have done for their parents in the past week. If the right column is longer than the left, I suggest that parents refrain from doing the extra things for their children until the columns even out a bit.

I suggest the following extreme interventions on the part of the parents if children are not being "kind to the vendors."

➤ If your child is disrespectful to you in front of the child's peers, end the outing by sending the peers home or taking your child home.

➤ If the child is behaving inappropriately or being highly demanding during any event, (i.e. sports activity, trip to the video store, shopping) put them in the car and take them home.

It does not matter where you are or what you are doing, even if they are about to start their baseball game or hockey practice. For most kids, this only needs to happen once or twice for them to learn to modify their behavior. Trust me. There is absolutely no activity that is more important than parents clearly setting limits in regards to how their children will be allowed to treat them.

Category Three: If you mess it up, you clean it up. And, you clean it up with the person(s) with whom you messed it up. This is one of the most useful interventions in regards to helping children and teens appreciate the full impact of their behavior on others; thereby increasing their empathy for others.

I often talk to distraught parents who are mortified by a particular behavior on the part of their child. This is often behavior that has affected others in a negative way. The first response many parents have is to rush in and fix the situation. The following is an example of this consequence.

I consulted with a parent who hosted a party for her young adolescent daughter. The daughter made arrangements to obtain alcohol and several of her guests drank. When the mother discovered what happened she took appropriate action and grounded her daughter. Her next step was to call the parents of the other children and inform them about what had happened. While it was certainly appropriate and brave to make sure the other parents were notified, I suggested she add another dimension to the consequence for her daughter. I recommended that she have her daughter call up each parent and apologize for her actions. I knew that "cleaning up her mess" with those parents would provide more of a lasting impact than grounding alone. The mother followed my advice, and found that several unexpected benefits came from these phone calls. Most parents the child talked to, knew the child well, and had in-depth conversations during which they discussed, in a very nurturing manner, their concerns about her behavior. This increased accountability, but also served as additional support for the child and the mothers. This served to increase this young lady's attachments to others in her world.

One might ask, what if the adults had not responded in such a nurturing and positive way? Welcome to the real world. When we make choices, we do need to think about the possible responses of others. Sometimes, others will not be so understanding; another lesson to be learned.

When my oldest son was young, we had a teenage baby sitter from our neighborhood. She sent my son to his room early in the evening, and asked some friends over without our permission. We returned home a bit early, and noticed a car in the drive that did not belong there. And, we returned home to a very upset young child. When I notified the girl's mother, she was horrified and informed me that she intended to ground her daughter. I requested that she send her daughter back to my house for a little chat with my husband and me.

The babysitter returned and quickly refunded our money. When I asked her to step inside, she became uncomfortable. We had a short discussion of how her behavior impacted our family. We were not harsh, but we were serious. The mother called me later and shared that she did not know what we had said to her daughter, but whatever it was impacted her far more than the grounding alone.

Confident Parenting In A Complex World-

Category Four: If you take something, you give back what you took, and you give back an equal amount extra. This is the primary consequence we suggest for stealing. It goes without saying that the child or teen needs to return whatever they took. The additional step, which involves giving back an equal amount extra, allows for the child to develop an understanding of the significance of what they have taken.

I once worked with an adolescent male who was diagnosed with Bipolar Mood Disorder. Whenever he was in a manic phase, he was prone to steal. I received a call from his father saying that his son had taken a large sum of money from a parent of one of his son's friends. The money had been returned and the other parent had agreed that he would not press legal charges, but the father was at a loss for what type of consequence he should give his son. I recommended that the teen offer a face to face apology and volunteer to work for the man, doing yard work and odd jobs, at a minimum wage rate, until it equaled the amount that he had taken. By the end of the consequence, this teen had an entirely new appreciation for the significance of the amount of money he had taken.

By giving up something of theirs of equal value, the child appreciates the significance of what they have taken from someone else.

While counseling with a young child, she stole cherished Pokemon cards from her younger cousin. She not only had to return the cards, she had to give her cousin one of her most cherished cards. Shortly after that, the child stole money from another family member. She had to return the money taken, and give up her allowance until she matched the amount that she took, then offer that to the family member, as well. After the second incident, the child did not

-Value Based Consequences

steal again.

Giving back what has been taken can take several forms. For example, if the child is constantly disrupting a family activity or making the family late for work, school, or other events, the child can give "time" back to the family, in the form of work or assistance.

Category Five: If you break something, you fix it. If you cannot fix it, you have to make arrangements to get it fixed. If someone has to fix it for you, you need to do something nice for the person who fixed it for you.

One of my best friends shared this story with me.

Her mild mannered adolescent son became very upset with his highly spirited younger sister. He became agitated, struck the wall and left a hole in it. He promptly tried to avoid responsibility for his actions by blaming his "very annoying" sister, since she had pushed him to that point. His mother insisted that he take responsibility for his behavior. He had to make arrangements for the wall to be repaired. He called workmen, got estimates, checked references, waited at home for them to come, and then paid for the work with his own money. Throughout this consequence he repeatedly implored his mother, "Please, can't you just ground me like a normal parent?"

Here's another example.

I worked with a young man who became agitated on a school field trip and proceeded to cause significant damage to the school bus. The school called me to inform me of their intention to suspend him for his behavior. I urged the school to provide another consequence as an option. The student was told he had the option of spending a Saturday working at the facility that maintained the school buses. Since someone else had to spend time repairing his damage, he would in turn spend time cleaning buses. He was told that if he chose to serve the consequence, he would not be suspended. Initially the young man stated that he had no intention of working all day Saturday, but he ultimately chose the consequence. He actually told me later he really liked the gentleman who maintains the buses he worked with that day, and felt bad he had created so much work for him.

My favorite story involving the "and if you break it, fix it" consequence:

A young man became very angry with a neighbor and decided to destroy her mailbox. The mom suggested they call me, and come up with an appropriate consequence. The teen was opposed to calling me, and suggested that he simply pay the neighbor for the cost of a new mail box. The mom felt that the consequence was appropriate, provided the young man hand deliver the payment and make a face to face apology. The young man offered to pay twice the amount of the mailbox, as long as he did not have to offer a face to face apology. The mother stood firm on the issue. I was amazed at the length the young man was willing to go in order to avoid accountability for how his actions had impacted others. Clearly, the face to face apology was a very important part of the learning experience for this teen.

Category Six: If you do something mean, you have to do something nice for the person to whom you did something mean. Note, I did not say you SAY something nice, I said you DO something nice. It is too easy for a child or teen to mouth the words of apology, with no sincerity attached to them. Indeed, "Just kidding," is usually the

-Value Based Consequences

automatic response most teens and children give, when confronting with hurtful words. This consequence is easy to implement, and self explanatory. It is the consequence we most often recommend for sibling rivalry.

There are a few important points to keep in mind when utilizing this consequence. I usually recommend that the "something nice" action take the form of something helpful, as well as something positive. It is usually my hope that the consequence will actually improve the relationship between the child and the person to whom the child was mean. I much prefer consequences that require children to do things like:

➤ *Read a story to a younger sibling.*

➤ *Drive a sibling to an event.*

➤ *Watch a sibling's sporting event, choir concert, or play.*

➤ *Help a sibling with their homework.*

➤ *Assist a sibling in organizing their room.*

These are activities that encourage more positive involvement in the lives of those around them. Doing chores for a sibling or family member is an acceptable consequence, but is certainly less positive than the previously mentioned actions.

In this category, I strongly discourage consequences that are monetary, such as buying the sibling something, or giving the sibling money. I also discourage consequences that are highly negative or punitive, such as requiring the child to do a particularly unpleasant job. When using this as a consequence for sibling rivalry, I encourage parents to decide on the consequence, as opposed to asking the sibling to decide. This allows adults to control the tone.

I often suggest parents use this consequence when their children act in a way that disregards mom or dad's feelings. For example, if a teen stays out past curfew and the parent has been awake worrying, I might suggest the teen do work for the parent the next day, to allow the parent to catch up on their sleep by sleeping in late, or by taking a nap.

Parents might find it helpful to follow the technique developed by a friend of mine who is an elementary school teacher. She had her students come up with a list of nice things others could do for them. She put these items in a jar. When a student would do something mean, she would have that student pull one of the items out of the jar. This helped her have an instant supply of consequences to call upon when the situation arose.

Selecting the Correct Category

It is not unusual for parents to feel stumped when trying to think about the most appropriate consequences for a specific behavior. In order to make this process easier for parents, I suggest parents simply ask themselves the following questions, and follow the next steps:

1. What is the specific behavior that I am trying to address? Isolate the behavior. Consequences work best when we are reacting to a specific incident versus a general behavior pattern. "The child steals," is too general. "The child took a toy from the home of a friend," is specific. "The child is destructive," is too general. "The child broke a window," is specific. "The child is mean to his brother," is general. "The child shoved his brother, and called him a name," is specific.

2. Is this an "other-directed" behavior? In other words,

-Value Based Consequences

does the behavior I am addressing with my child involve an act that impacts other people? These types of consequences are more effective with behavior that involves an "other." They do not work as well for behavior that primarily affects the child, (like not doing their homework).

3. Which of the six categories best describes the behavior?

(Do not be surprised if several categories seem to fit.)

A. If you abuse it, you lose it.
B. Be kind to the vendor.
C. If you mess it up, you clean it up.
D. If you take something, return it double.
E. If you break it you fix it.
F. If you do something mean, you do something nice.

4. Select a category.

5. Decide on a consequence.

6. If the child refuses to accept the consequence, then combine a take away, with a give back. In other words, calmly inform the child, "That's up to you; however, until this consequence is complete, you will not be allowed to_____."

7. Walk away. Do not warn, threaten, argue or discuss. In most situations, children do not choose to ignore the consequence. They just want to see what kind of reaction they can elicit from you by threatening not to comply. By walking away, parents avoid temptation to engage in a nonproductive power struggle with their child. Walking away also prevents an escalation of conflict.

In a recent parent group, one of the fathers found the six categories so helpful that he put them on posters and displayed them throughout the house.

Consequences Over a Period of Time

In recent years we have focused on parenting techniques that provide quick and simple interventions to stop inappropriate behavior. The philosophy behind these interventions is that we should address the behavior, provide an immediate short term intervention (such as a time-out), and go back to the daily routine of the family, without wasting a lot of time and energy focusing on the misbehavior. While this approach is very appropriate and adequate for much of the minor day to day behavior that children display, there are behaviors that warrant more attention and require a different level of intensity and focus. Five minute time-outs do not provide the solution to every problem displayed by children. In fact, some behaviors require consequences of longer duration and substance. When trying to determine which behaviors require something more than a time-out, the following should be considered:

➤ *Behavior that is extreme in nature.*

➤ *Behavior that violates the core values of the family.*

➤ *Behavior that habitually continues or escalates in spite of the short term interventions.*

➤ *Behavior that is inappropriate for the child's age.*

➤ *Behavior that directly affects another in a negative or hurtful way.*

➤ *Whenever utilizing consequences other than time-outs, grounding or removing privileges provide a better learning*

-Value Based Consequences

experience.

These behaviors warrant a well thought out, creative, and somewhat unpredictable response. Parents often have trouble coming up with effective consequences while they are engaged in a conflict with their children. I often tell parents not to worry. If they miss an opportunity to give a strong consequence, they will probably have another chance in the near future.

The next time you find yourself dishing out a consequence that you feel is weak and ineffective for a behavior that is making you crazy, my advice is to give it some thought. Talk to someone about it, and come up with a plan for what you will be able to do next time.

In fact, if you are baffled about what to do, it is perfectly okay to tell your child, "Boy, I'm not sure what I'm going to do about this. I will definitely have to give this some thought. I'll get back to you when I decide." Giving it some thought, is a response that often makes kids nervous. They know if you give them an immediate response, you will be predictable and easier to manipulate. If you give it some thought, they do not have quite as much power.

One of my adolescent clients came into my office and reported that she was in big trouble with her parents because of something she had done. When I ask her what her parents planned to do, she responded, "I don't know. They said they are going to have to think about it. This is making me crazy. I don't know what they are going to do, but I have a feeling I am not going to like it! If I had known they were going to act like this, I would have thought more about what I did, before I did it."

Deliver Consequences with Empathy

When it comes to children learning lessons of life, actions always speak louder than words. One of the problems we have when disciplining our children is that we talk too much. We lecture, preach, threaten and warn. Many of us were raised by parents who did not explain crap to us, so we explain the crap out of everything. Talking too much inevitably leads to conflict, especially with adolescents. The conflict, not the child's behavior, becomes the focus.

If you allow your children to make choices, hold them responsible for their choices. Do not lecture, discuss, warn or threaten. In fact, for consequences to have the most impact, they should be delivered with kindness.

A teenager comes home with poor grades. The understanding between the teen and the parent is that the teenager will only have use of the car as long as grades are "C" or above.

The consequence is definite. The teen loses use of the car. However, the consequence can be delivered in anger or in empathy.

The first example illustrates anger.

"Well, we warned you about this. We tried to help you. We asked if you were keeping up with your school work, and you out and out lied to us, and told us 'yes.' You will not be allowed to drive the car until your grades are up. Maybe someday you'll learn to be responsible. I hope you think about this. Maybe this will motivate you. I hope so, because otherwise you'll be working at McDonald's all your life."

-Value Based Consequences

The focus here quickly becomes the conflict. Teens are insulted by this type of response. They feel their parents are putting them down, and treating them like they are stupid.

They either withdraw from the lecture or fight back. They feel their parents are mean, unfair, and uncaring. What's more, the teen's pride gets in the way. Teens are likely to respond defensively by retorting they don't care that they won't get to drive; they didn't like driving that much anyway. This false apathy makes parents crazy. It sends parents into the therapist's office announcing, "That kid just does not care about anything. It's impossible to motivate him!!!"

At this point, I suggest the parents relax. I have never known a kid who received an effective consequence, to respond with, "Ouch, that really hurt. That was good and effective consequence. Keep up the good work, Dad."

Let's look at dispensing the consequence with empathy.

"Well, our agreement is that you can drive the car as long as your grades are "C" or above, so you'll have to hand over the keys. That's a real bummer, I'm sure. Boy, I remember when I was a teenager, being able to drive was one of the best parts about being in high school. Having the freedom to get around without depending on your parents for a ride, and picking up your girlfriend. I'm really sorry you're going to miss out on that, but I know you'll get your grades up next semester. You're a smart kid."

This dialogue keeps the focus on the issue at hand, the grades and the car. Because it is empathetic instead of hostile, it really encourages the teen to think about the loss of driving privileges, instead of how the parents talked to them. It results in less conflict, fewer bad feelings, and less rebellion on the part of the teen.

Deliver consequences with kindness. It increases the impact.

Consequences of Attachment

Often in our search for the most effective consequence, we make a serious error. We look for what is most important to the child, and we threaten to take it away. There are several problems with this approach. Very often, the thing we threaten to take away has nothing to do with the behavior we are trying to address; therefore, the consequence has a limited impact. The thing the child enjoys the most may be the main activity of competence, self esteem, and belonging for the child. To take away these critical components of the child's life will not help the child in the long run. The most important activity in the child's life may provide the child with his or her only positive primary social connections, important adult relationships and valuable skill development. There are many ways to discipline children without utilizing consequences that isolate and exclude children. In fact in this decade, when many children have fragile and tenuous attachments, we need to protect—not sever any attachments children do have with others.

The following are examples of adults utilizing detachment, isolation, and exclusion based consequences.

A college friend of mine has a beautiful daughter who was in her early teens. As a young child, she struggled with school because she had learning disabilities. These struggles created difficulty for her because she believed she was stupid. She was isolated socially, and her self esteem was very poor. When she was in fourth grade, she began to play the violin. She discovered that she was incredibly talented at this instrument. As her skill in this area improved, she transformed into a confident, social, well-connected, young lady with a goal of being a concert violinist. She explained that other people looked up to her because of her talent, that she never questioned herself when she played, and that she had many adults who were devoted to her. She had a mission, a meaning, and a purpose.

During her seventh grade year, her math teacher became concerned that her math grade was a "C." He called a conference in which he suggested to the mother that perhaps if this young lady spent less time on the violin, and more time on math, her grade would improve. He further suggested that perhaps her mother should restrict her from the violin for the semester.

The fact is, this young lady made poor grades in math before she began playing the violin. The math and the violin had no connection to one another. To take this child's violin away would not be a consequence that made any sense. It would only serve to isolate the child from her support network, and focus on her weakness, not her strength. It was a poor idea for a consequence. I suggested to my friend that there were many things to take away to address the math grade, like the phone or the TV, without implementing a consequence of isolation.

Most high schools have policies on zero tolerance for alcohol and drug use among their athletes. The policies very simply state that athletes who are caught using alcohol and/or drugs will be kicked off the team. While this is a consequence that certainly holds teens responsible, it is also a consequence of exclusion. I would venture to say that students who are kicked off the team will not be around during game time to see and feel what they are missing. In fact, they will most likely be out using the alcohol or the drugs that got them suspended in the first place.

The problem with this consequence is that when people are under the influence, they do not spend much time while using thinking about consequences. I often suggest an alternative consequence. When student athletes are caught drinking or using, try to implement a consequence that meets some of the criteria we discussed earlier (it requires some effort on the part of the child, it encourages the child to think about their decision, and it takes place over a period of time). I suggest we give the teens choices. Give them the choice to remain on the team. However, if this is their choice, they must complete a substance abuse assessment, and at the very least, participate in a drug and alcohol education group.

I do not necessarily believe alcohol and/or drug education groups always stop the teen's drug use, but it gives a clear message that we take this very seriously. At best, it will be helpful; at worst it will be boring. Either way, it requires some effort, as well as time commitment. In addition, the teen would be required to attend and participate in all the practices and show up for the games, which would be spent on the bench. That teen will think a great deal about poor choices, while sitting on the bench watching his or her teammates play.

I have counseled many addicted adolescents during my career. There was a time, for most of them, that they had some connections to positive peer cultures and activities. Once these connections were severed, they moved further and further into negative drug using cultures. The more deeply involved they became in these cultures, the more difficult it was for them to give up their drugs and rebuild their lives.

-Value Based Consequences

Consequences of exclusion tend to further alienate and isolate kids who are at risk of detaching themselves from the family, schools, communities and activities. Consequences that promote this process are not helpful, and in many cases are actually harmful.

Life Is a Good Teacher

Some of the most valuable lessons children learn are from the logical and natural consequences of life. Sometimes parents are so busy parenting that they get in the way of their child's learning from life. Parents rescue their children, bail them out, come to their defense, make excuses for them, or indulge them, without expecting them to put forth any effort

I see parents heartbroken and exhausted, because they have done everything they can think of to help their children, but their children continue to make poor choices. Everything they can think of often includes bailing them out of jail, rescuing them from difficult teachers, paying for attorneys. The problem is that they are "too" helpful. So helpful, that those children never learn, never pay the price, and never grow up.

The amazing thing about most of our children is that they do not need to be rescued. However, they will never know this if parents rescue them whether they need it or not. Children whose parents rescue them from life's consequences consistently tell me the same things.

➤ *They are insulted because they feel their parents think they are incompetent to handle things on their own.*

➤ *They continue to get into trouble because they would like their parents to allow them to fail, just once, so they can pick themselves up and move on.*

➤ *As one very astute seventeen year old once told me, "My parents keep asking me when I am going to learn. Maybe I would learn if they quit going to school to bail me out of trouble all the time."*

➤ *They have no confidence in themselves because they have not had an opportunity to prove to themselves that they can handle their lives.*

➤ *They are angry at their parents and their parents do not understand why. They are tired of their parents lecturing and warning them, especially since they do not believe their parents will follow through with any of these warnings.*

Instead of rescuing our children, our energy would be better spent discussing possible choices and very calmly walking them through the probable outcome of these choices. Then, walking away and letting them mull it over. Very often, parents do not need to intervene; they merely need to let natural consequences take their course.

Allowing life to be a teacher often requires that we get out of the way, and let life take over. I have a friend who is a teacher. She is a dedicated professional who is fair and very concerned about the welfare of her students. She believes that in addition to teaching English, it is her job to teach responsibility. She admits that with every four detentions she gives her students for inappropriate behavior, she gets two sets of parents calling her, or coming in to complain about her giving their children consequences. She admits she often thinks it would just be easier to let the kids off the hook. It would be easier on her, and easier on the parents. Unfortunately, it would be potentially harmful to the children.

-Value Based Consequences

Most children behave inappropriately at school sometimes. They do not need us to rescue them from the consequences of inappropriate behavior. What will determine if misbehavior at school is an isolated incident vs. a long term pattern, depends largely on whether we rescue them or let them face the music.

Assume the Best

One of the reasons a child makes poor choices over and over again, is we assume the worst and proceed accordingly. We badger our children about their poor choices, lecture and warn about the consequences, and let them know we expect them to make another poor choice the next time. If we expect the worst in children, they will perform for us. I often ask parents, when was the last time they expected the best from their children. When children make mistakes, we can either assume the worst, "Next time don't expect me to bail you out," or assume the best, "I know you are a smart kid, and you will make a better choice next time." Sometimes it is important to say this, even if you do not believe it. Parents are much more likely to encourage appropriate behavior when they take the positive approach, as opposed to the negative.

Beyond the Home

As our cultural orientation toward parenting has changed, our communities, schools and legal systems have also changed. We are much more likely to encounter systems today that do not hold children responsible. In addition, many of the systems that deal with children would rather take an easy approach (i.e. kick the kids out of class) as opposed to an effective approach (i.e. give the kids consequences that will require some effort on their part) that may perhaps teach the children a lesson.

Once parents have completed my seminars, they often find themselves at odds with the systems that deal with their children.

One set of parents came to parent group and reported that the school counselor told them I could write an excuse for their daughter, which would allow her to drop out of chemistry without penalty, as opposed to failing the class. The parents were confused by this because they felt that this was a direct contradiction of what I had been teaching them. I informed them I would not write this letter, because there was no reason for their child to be flunking chemistry. The parents agreed with me. We found ourselves dealing with a very confused, concerned, and overly helpful school counselor.

I had been working with a young man who had numerous learning and emotional problems. Both he and his parents had made significant progress.

Then the young man made a poor choice in an industrial class. He misused a tool in direct defiance of the teacher. The teacher wanted to kick him out of the class. The parents wanted to attack the school, because they had not made any accommodations for this young man's learning and emotional problems. The student was convinced he did not have to do anything to correct the situation, because he believed his mother was going to send him to a private school.

It was my opinion the school needed to modify their instruction to accommodate this student's special learning needs. That did not, however, excuse the young man's

-Value Based Consequences

highly inappropriate behavior. I suggested the young man be given a choice to remain in the class or not. If he chose to remain in class, he would need to have a discussion with the dean as well as his teacher, regarding the proper use of tools and the potential danger of misusing tools. In addition, he would be given a consequence wherein he would be responsible for the tools in class. This would involve making sure the tools were put away at the end of each class, as well as time after school or during study hall, to complete service work in the class. There was a great deal of discussion, and everyone thought it was a good idea. However, several people let it be known that while they felt the consequence would be more beneficial for this young man, kicking him out of class would just be a lot easier.

We as a culture are paying a huge price for taking the easy way out with children. When we work together as a culture, the impact on children is highly beneficial.

One of my sons is very opinionated and strong willed. When he was five years old, he decided he knew most of what there was to know about the world. Needless to say, no amount of arguing could teach him otherwise. At one point, he decided in the middle of winter that he did not want to wear his coat to school. He did not want to give an explanation. He simply put up a huge stink in the mornings. One morning when it was uncomfortably cold, but not freezing, he began his resistance to wearing his coat. I decided I was not going to fight this battle. I informed him that I planned to wear my coat because I did not want to get cold. He insisted he would not wear his coat, so I allowed him to make this very poor choice. Once we were in the car, he commented that he was cold and wanted his coat. I told him that I was really sorry that he was cold, but reminded him that he had left his coat at home. He was quite indignant, and told me I should have brought it because he is just a little boy, and I should have known he might change his mind. He then told me he did not like to wear his coat, because it got too warm running around on the playground. I informed him he would not have that problem today, since children who do not wear coats are not allowed outside to play. When we arrived at school, the teacher looked at me in disbelief when she asked my son where his coat was, and I replied to her he had "chosen" not to wear his coat. This very wise teacher recognized this was a learning experience. She explained to us he would not be allowed to go on the playground without a coat. When playground time rolled around, my son eagerly lined up. He was astonished and very disappointed when the teacher reminded him he could not go out. He never argued about the coat again.

Some people confuse control with good parenting. I certainly could have forced my son to put his coat on, and we could have battled every morning. However, I could never have convinced my son through arguing, that when he is asked to do something, I have his own well being in mind. By allowing him to make poor choices, he learns that perhaps he does not know everything there is to know about the world, and that there are often good reasons for the rules and expectations. This is a lesson that arguing, lecturing, and threatening cannot teach.

I am impressed by schools that have excellent policies in place, which require the children to take responsibility for their actions.

We have a local high school that realizes it is futile and ineffective to utilize suspension for teens who are truant from school. Teens often say they make sure the school knows when they intentionally skip school, because the consequence is an out of school suspension. They feel like it

-Value Based Consequences

is a vacation day, not in any way a deterrent to future truancy. Instead, the teens are required to serve an out of school detention at a local adolescent detention center. The teens complain about this, but it has been effective in reducing truancy. The only catch is that the program places a hardship on the parents because they are expected to provide transportation. The school starts at 8:00 AM and ends at 3:00 PM, so many parents found themselves missing work because of the poor choices their children made. I suggested parents give their teens two choices. Either go to school on the parents' way to work and wait at the end of the day until the parents are on their way home, or take a cab at their own expense. This added twist increased the effectiveness of the consequence, and gave an even more powerful statement to the teens about responsibility.

Timing is Everything

As all parents know, sometimes we do not have time to implement a consequence on the spot because we are in a hurry or the situation does not offer us the opportunity. That's okay, we do not have to react, we can chose our time

I recently had a mom complain that the minute her children got in the car, a sibling battle would ensue. Often, she was on her way to taking them to school, and then going to work, and could not turn the car around, or pull off to the side of the road, because of her time schedule. With some planning and forethought, she decided the next time her children were in the car headed for a recreational event of some sort, she would without a word, turn the car around and head for home the minute they started arguing. She soon got to implement this consequence. The children were shocked and employed all the manipulation techniques children use in an attempt to change their mother's mind.

Although she was tempted to give in, lecture them and warn them, she stood her ground. She was very firm and empathic. She told them she understood how disappointing it must be to miss a birthday party, especially one as great as this one. She refrained from lecturing the children on what they had done wrong, and telling them she hoped they had learned a good lesson. The children were quite shocked and the sibling battles in the car came to an end.

Here is another example.

Recently, a very bewildered and frustrated father of an extremely emotional adolescent female walked into my office in somewhat of a daze. He was obviously upset. When I asked him what had happened, he informed me that while on the way to my office for their appointment, his daughter had gotten completely out of control in the car. She began yelling and screaming, threatening to strike him. Although his first impulse was to strike her out of frustration, he remembered the things we had discussed in parent group about consequences. Since he could not come up with a consequence on the spot and continue to drive, he pulled the car over. He took the keys and began walking, as he tried to think of a good consequence. He walked all the way to my office, and was still bewildered about what he should do about the situation.

As we were discussing it, his daughter sheepishly appeared at my office door. Her only comment was to look at her dad and say, "Nice Dad, leave me stranded in the middle of the city." However, she never repeated that behavior. By just stepping back and trying to find a solution, her father accidentally happened upon a very effective consequence.

When we are faced with recurring behavioral challenges

-Value Based Consequences

with children sometimes we need to step back, reflect, think and plan, before we implement. By doing this we can remove ourselves from the emotional craziness of the moment and can become actors instead of reactors. When we are actors, we are able to maintain control over ourselves, our situations, and our emotions. Actors often puzzle children, because they are not as predictable; therefore, not quite as easy to manipulate.

Often adults, teachers, parents, and professionals get caught in power struggles regarding consequences. People often ask what to do if they give a consequence, and their child refuses to accept it. Adults want to know how to respond when a child says, "What happens if I don't?" Once again, do not feel you have to come up with the answer immediately. My favorite answer in such situations is, "That's a good question. I am not sure what I will do. Boy, I am going to have to give that some thought. Yeah, that one will need a lot of thought. I might even have to talk to someone else about that. I'll let you know what I decide. In the mean time, you give some thought to what I asked you to do, and let me know what you decide." With that, I walk away. It is very important to realize children are more interested in what you will do if they threaten to not cooperate, than they are in not cooperating.

Very often, children will comply with what was asked of them if we simply walk away without arguing, lecturing, threatening or trying to cajole. I often used this approach when I worked in residential treatment with teenagers. I asked a young man to do something. He asked what would happen if he did not. Another group member jumped in and said, "Look, with her you never know what will happen, but I can tell you one thing, you won't like it!"

Confident Parenting In A Complex World-

I once worked with a family whose fourteen year old daughter would fly into rages when she did not get her way, or when she was bored. The parents became very skilled at responding to her rages in an effective way. She decided they were no fun, so she began to direct her rages at her younger brother and sister. This would result in the entire household being in a state of crisis and chaos. After several of these episodes, the parents decided the next time this happened they would leave the house and take the two younger children with them. They planned to participate in an enjoyable family outing. They planned in advance for a family friend to come stay with the fourteen year old. They also planned to pay this person as a babysitter, and have the fourteen year old pay the bill. If the outburst happened at night, they planned to leave and get a hotel room, for which they intended to have the fourteen year old pay. They had an agreement with the family friend, who said she could stay the night, if necessary. With this plan in place, the family eagerly awaited the next outburst. It never came. When talking to the fourteen year old in therapy, she told me she decided she had better watch her temper; her parents were getting too weird, and she never knew what they were going to pull next. She also confided in me that she had the impression they were up to something.

Parents of teens often report when they try to implement a consequence of restriction teens become defiant and refuse to cooperate. Conflicts often escalate to a physical level. Parents will report they asked their child to turn over the car keys or turn over their cell phones. When these requests are met with defiance, parents either walk away, because they don't know how to respond, or engage in a physical conflict in attempt to obtain the items. Neither of these responses places the parent in control of the situation.

I coach parents to step back from the situation in the moment, and think about ways to ramp up accountability so that teens realize defiance results in serious consequences.

For example, if teens refuse to turn over cell phones, I recommend that parents simply contact their phone company and have the service turned off. If the teens refuse to turn over the car keys or if they continually ignore limits parents impose on the car, I suggest that parents wait until their child is in bed, get in the car and drive it to a location unknown to the teen. The car remains there until parents feel the teens are ready to have access to the car.

These consequences provide ultimate boundaries for the child, provide a clear message that defiance will not be tolerated and will cause significant consequences.

An Emotional, Behavioral or Learning Diagnosis

I have talked to several parents who agree with the philosophy of utilizing consequences as a form of discipline, but are confused about implementing consequences because their children have been diagnosed with mood issues, ADHD or Bipolar disorders. When children with clinical diagnoses display behavioral problems, parents question, "Is this their disorder, or is this intentional misbehavior?" The answer is, "Both." Most children I have met in therapy, who behave inappropriately, tell me they could have controlled their behavior better if they had chosen to do so.

It is important to remember that all kids are kids first. They are kids, before they are a diagnosis. One of the best things about utilizing consequences as discipline is that the focus is on accountability and learning vs. punishment. All children, regardless of their diagnosis, need to learn that they are held accountable for their behavior.

For example, ADHD children are sometimes a bit accident prone and will knock things over and break things. When questioned about such things, they typically respond with "I'm sorry." and, "It was an accident." They probably are sorry, and it probably was an accident. In spite of that, it will likely happen again. Regardless of the fact this behavior is part of the child's disorder, something has been broken and the person who broke it must be the one who takes the responsibility to get it fixed. Children with psychiatric and clinical diagnoses are children who need to learn they are expected to manage their choices, or like everyone else, be held accountable for their choices. We are, of course, here to give them any assistance they need to develop coping skills. In this process, we must not forget that taking responsibilty for one's actions is in fact one of these coping skills.

CHAPTER THREE
Dealing with Dishonesty

Dishonesty in Children and Teens

One of the most concerning problems parents seek advice about is dishonesty. Dishonesty does not fit easily into the value based consequence model we discussed in the previous chapter. Therefore, I have chosen to devote a separate chapter to this issue.

Parents often become distressed the first time they realize their child has been dishonest with them. This usually occurs around the age of five. Parents question, "Why would they do this?" The answer is simple. It's because their brains have matured enough that they realize they can. Most kids lie in attempt to solve a problem.

Unfortunately most, if not all kids, lie to their parents at some point. There are different types of lies and while lying is never good, some forms of dishonesty are more unhealthy than others. When deciding the best way to intervene or prevent dishonesty, it is important to identify what type of dishonesty your child is displaying.

Lying to avoid being in trouble, is by far the most common type of deception practiced by children. As long as there are children who do things that result in disapproval from adults, there will be children who lie to adults to avoid their disapproval, as well as possible consequences of this disapproval.

One of the simplest and most effective ways to prevent this type of dishonesty is to follow the rule, "If you know, don't ask." What parent is not guilty of asking a question to which they already have the answer? For example, we listen outside the bathroom while the child prepares for school and we know beyond a shadow of a doubt they did not brush their teeth. The first thing we say when they emerge is, "Did you brush your teeth?" If you look closely enough, you will see their wheels spinning as they quickly evaluate their options. The child thinks, "They don't know if I did or not. If I tell them no, they are probably going to get mad and lecture me, then I will have to go back and brush my teeth, and I hate brushing my teeth!" After careful consideration, the child looks up and says, "Yes." The response typically enrages parents because the child has made matters worse by being dishonest. Parents typically come back at the child with, "I know you did not brush your teeth, and how can you stand there and lie to me?" If you look closely at the child's face you can imagine what they are thinking. It probably goes something like this, "Well if you knew, why did you ask me in the first place?"

Don't test children beyond where their moral development and maturity takes them. Avoiding an angry or upset adult is a strong motivator for children to be less than honest.

The following are tips are designed to promote honesty and discourage lying in children and teens that are avoiding getting in trouble.

➤ "If you know, don't ask." To utilize the previous example, if you know your child did not brush his/her teeth, simply state, "You did not brush your teeth. Please take care of that now." Or you could say, "There is something you forgot. Can you think of what it was?"

➤ Be straight forward; don't play "cops and robbers." Parents often feel compelled to trap kids into confessing dishonesty by backing them into a corner with questions. This serves no purpose other than to promote kids lying to cover up lies, and creating nonproductive and hostile interaction. The following scenario often gets reported in

Dealing With Dishonesty

my office.

An adolescent lies to their parents and tells them they have gone to a movie. The parents discover the child did not go to the movie and start the grand inquisition that goes something like this, "So, how was the movie? Who was there? What was it about? Are you sure you went? Maybe I'll call___ ___ and ask them if they saw you there." By the end of this line of questioning, everyone is angry. The more the kid lies, the more they get locked into defending their story.

I suggest skipping all the drama and getting to the point with, "We know you did not go to the movies, so let's talk about where you did go."

➤ Don't support them digging themselves a hole. Once kids and teens tell a lie, they feel compelled to lock in and defend the lie. The more they talk, the more they lie, and the more angry parents become. At this point trying to convince them to tell the truth is futile. The most productive course of action is to simply stop the discussion for the time being. This can be accomplished by calmly stating, "Stop. We are not going to continue to discuss this. You need to take some time and think about this and when you are ready to be honest, let me know." Or saying, "Stop. Don't respond right now. Take a breath and don't talk again unless you are prepared to tell the truth."

If you feel that a consequence is appropriate, then you can add one on. For example, "Until we have an honest discussion about this, I am not going to be comfortable allowing you to go out with your friends," (or whatever is appropriate for the situation).

➤ **Implement a grace period.** Unfortunately, when children and teens have established a pattern of consistently lying, lying becomes a habit. Often, children and teens will lie for absolutely no reason. They will lie when the truth would be easier, even when the truth carries no risk of consequence. In these situations, kids lie automatically and feel like the dishonesty is out of their mouth before they have even had time to think about it. Once the dishonesty is out, they compulsively lie to cover up. The goal, in these situations, is to help children and teens disrupt the cycle. One way to do that is to implement a grace period or a "make it okay" loop. This is accomplished by having a calm discussion with your child about their dishonesty. Calm discussions usually go best when you are not dealing with an active situation of dishonesty. In other words, approach the subject at a neutral time, not when the child is "in trouble" for lying. Discuss your observation that your child appears to be lying automatically. Share that as a family, you have to find a solution to this problem. Therefore, you are implementing a penalty-free zone. If the child tells a lie, they will be given a 15 minute period in which they can come back and correct the lie without consequences or punishment for the dishonesty. If, however, you discover they lied, there will be a consequence.

This approach allows the child an opportunity to break out of their pattern of compulsive dishonesty. I encourage parents to tackle this issue as soon as they are aware of it. The longer the pattern exists, the more difficult it is to correct.

Lying to Solve or Avoid Problems

Unfortunately, some children and teens absolutely hate it when others are upset with them. They are highly sensitive

Dealing With Dishonesty

to disappointing others and are very uncomfortable with any type of conflict. These children are masters of the false agreement. They are often internally conflicted. They want to do what they want to do, but they don't want others to be upset with them. Their solution to this internal conflict is to pretend to agree with adults, tell adults what they want to hear, then go and do whatever they want to do. They think they have stumbled onto the perfect solution. This works for them until their dishonesty is discovered. When those around them discover the deception, it creates havoc in their relationships. Unfortunately, instead of learning necessary skills for conflict resolution and relationship building, they utilize dishonesty as their main relationship tool and problem-solving skill. The younger children are when they begin this process, the more deeply ingrained it becomes. Often, by adolescence, the behavior becomes highly problematic as teens begin lying to closest friends, boyfriends and girlfriends, in much the same manner as they lie to their parents.

In order to help children and teens overcome this pattern, parents can discuss with them the following points.

➤ When you deceive people to avoid problems or solve problems, you come to depend on dishonesty as your main tool. It is important to learn other, better ways to manage relationships.

➤ When people discover you have lied to them, they feel angry and embarrassed they believed and trusted a person who lied to them.

➤ Sometimes people lie because they don't want others to be mad at them. Lying makes others mad and results in others distancing themselves from you.

➤ Most people eventually figure out when they are being lied to. It is foolish to continue to lie, when people don't believe you anyway.

➤ Trust people. Realize you can tell them the truth, even if the truth might create conflict. Friendships and relationships are strong enough to survive conflict, but not strong enough to survive dishonesty.

➤ Have you ever had someone lie to you? Do you remember how it felt? Do you remember what you thought about that person? Is that how you want people to think about you?

Inventing Tales and Exaggerating

Many children and teens lie in the form of embellishing a story or exaggerating an interaction, experience or situation. Young children will invent tales as an extension of their play. Teens will embellish or exaggerate to enhance their image or entertain others. These patterns are not particularly problematic as long as they occur infrequently and are connected to the child's or teen's reality. Parents can simply intervene by pointing out to the child their "story" is in full fantasy or commenting to teens and preteens (never in front of others) that their story appeared to be a bit of an exaggeration.

Habitual and Pathological Lying

Habitual and pathological dishonesty is different than previously discussed forms of dishonesty in children and teens. Pathological dishonesty is a serious problem that involves a chronic and persistent pattern of communicating with adults and peers. Children and teens that lie habitually,

Dealing With Dishonesty

often convince themselves they are, in fact, telling the truth. The longer this behavior persists, the more deeply ingrained it becomes and the more difficult it is to change.

Habitual lying can take several forms, including:

➤ Excessive amounts of lying to get out of trouble, avoid problems, impress others, and manipulate outcomes or getting one's way.

➤ Lying for absolutely no reason.

➤ Telling intentional lies about others. This may take the form of accusing someone of harming them.

➤ Inventing stories that have no basis in reality.

➤ Misperceiving and misinterpreting the actions, attitudes or intentions of others.

➤ Intentionally and maliciously telling lies about others.

This could be in the form of spreading rumors or lying to get someone in trouble. In such circumstances, dishonesty becomes a weapon, a threat, or a way to control others.

Pathological lying is actually fairly rare in children and teens. However, it is an issue of grave concern and may be a symptom of a psychological disorder. Parents can help their children by:

➤ Consistently and directly confronting the dishonesty by calmly and firmly stating, "I know that is not true."

➤ Encouraging others to confront the child. When children

Confident Parenting In A Complex World-

habitually lie they eventually begin lying to friends, peers, extended family, teachers and other adults. If others do not confront the dishonesty, the behavior becomes worse because children think that others believe them. Parents can enlist the help of others by explaining to them that the child has developed a serious pattern of dishonesty which needs to be directly confronted by others. As hard as it might be, do not cover for, enable, or make excuses for the child's behavior.

➤ If you are aware that your child has been dishonest with others, have the child write a letter of apology in which they discuss the lie and tell the truth.

➤ Have your child keep a truth journal for one month. In the journal they keep track of times they have been honest with others, as well as times they have lied. When journaling, have them describe the following:

This is what I have been dishonest about.

_____
_____

This is how other people feel about me because of my dishonesty.

_____
_____

This is how I feel about myself when I am dishonest:

_____
_____

This is what I have been honest about:

_____
_____

Dealing With Dishonesty

This is how others feel about me when I am honest:

_____
_____
_____

This is how I feel about myself when I am honest:

_____
_____
_____

➤ Select a consequence for dishonesty and implement it every time. This might be the loss of a privilege (such as the cell phone, television, computer, etc.) or it might be a fine paid through actions, such as a designated chore or designated work time.

➤ Get help. If your child is chronically dishonest, it is time to seek the help of a therapist who can help your child change this pattern of behavior.

Fortunately, most dishonest behavior can be corrected as the child matures. As parents, it is important to intervene but not overreact.

CHAPTER FOUR

The Technologically Savvy Parent

The Most Recent Parenting Challenge

As if parenting is not confusing and challenging enough, we are now faced with parenting dilemmas for which we have no historical wisdom, little research, and limited guidance. I am, of course, referring to parenting in the age of technology. Technology has a significant impact on our children, and on our parenting of them. It is an issue that must be addressed when discussing value based parenting.

For the sake of simplicity, we will refer to the use of technology by our children as "screen time." When we view technology in this way, it is amazing how much screen time the average child or teen is exposed to during the course of a day, a week, a year or a lifetime. Screens refer to video and computer games, computer use, television and DVD viewing, movies, texting, cell phones, iPods, and hand held games. These screens are ever present and ever influential in our lives and the lives of our children.

We live in an age of technology. We cannot avoid, deny or ignore this fact. Raising children in this age requires we find ways to maneuver through this ever changing technological culture. As with all other parenting issues, we need to learn to set appropriate limits and boundaries, developing strategies to monitor our children as they integrate technology into their worlds. In order to do this, parents must understand any impact that technology has, both positive and negative, on development.

Screen Time and Development

Childhood and adolescent development is marked by a long series of social, emotional, behavioral and psychological tasks that must be addressed and mastered by children in order for them to competently transition from one age to the next, and from one phase to the next. Many of these tasks can only be mastered through the child's direct interaction with his/her world. Play, movement and interaction with others lay the ground work for developing skills such as social intelligence, conflict resolution, complex cognitive skills, empathy development, physical, and social competence. These developmental tasks are often difficult, complex, require a great deal of work, and are sometimes anxiety producing for the child, as well as for parents who watch their children struggle and wonder what they can do to assist them and perhaps make the path easier for them. Parents need to be vigilant in order to safe guard children from using screens to such an extent that development is compromised. Screens are beneficial if used to enhance a child's social world, but not when they are used as a substitute for the child's social life. They are of benefit when used to entertain, but not at the expense of other physical activities or real life activities. They are beneficial when used to enhance the child's world, but not when they become a mechanism to avoid the world.

Cognitive Development

The brain is the only organ in the body whose development is dependent on interaction with, and stimulation from, the environment. Therefore, a child's brain is significantly impacted by the types of activities in which children choose to engage.

At approximately age eleven, the brain produces an abundance of new gray matter in the cerebellum region. For years, researchers and brain experts assumed this part of the brain was only responsible for the development of physical grace and coordination. More recent research has shown that this region of the brain also contributes to social development. Development in this part of the brain assists individuals with social grace, maneuvering complex social situations, and in complex executive functioning. As with all gray matter, the brain maintains gray matter that it uses and it prunes out the rest. Simply stated, if one does not use it, one will lose it. Physical activity in the latter years of elementary school does a great deal to contribute to a child's ongoing social development as the child passes from childhood, and into adolescence.

As children are leaving elementary school and preparing to enter middle school, they need physical activity to insure healthy cognitive development.

This, unfortunately comes at a time when most children get less physical activity in their lives because:

➤ *Children no longer have recess or access to a play ground at school. In fact, most middle school children only have gym every other nine weeks, and much of that time is "sit" time vs. "movement" time.*

➤ *Many children drop out of organized sports, because at this age competition becomes more important than fun. Children find themselves getting cut from middle school teams, and withdrawing from recreational leagues, because the coaching becomes overly critical, the time commitments become unrealistic, and kids feel there is no sense in continuing if they cannot be competitive.*

➤ *Most schools and communities do not offer after school programs for middle school students. These programs typically encourage children to participate in physical activities.*

➤ Many middle school children come home after school to empty houses because their parents are at work. In order to ensure the child's safety, parents mandate that the children go home, go inside, lock the door and do not have friends over. Instead of being physically active, children fill their empty time with screens. The last thing these children and their brains need is more screen time, especially at the expense of physical activity.

Consequently, at a time which children desperately need physical activities, many avenues for such activity are not available. Many children are replacing physical activity with screen time.

Social Development

More screen time and less physical activity not only impair social development from a neurological basis, but it also impairs social development from an opportunity perspective.

During late elementary school and early middle school, social interaction becomes much more complex. Kids begin to develop more significant and closer relationships with peers. Kids begin developing best friends and they do this based on personality and preference vs. sheer convenience. As relationships become more intense, conflict becomes more common. The ability to understand and resolve these conflicts are critical. Kids seem to sense the significance of their social development at this age. Anyone who has spent any time with fourth and fifth graders knows that kids at this age seem obsessed about the status of their social relationships. Who does not remember the constant note sending at this age for the sole purpose of social reassurance? My own late elementary school years were filled with notes containing the following:

Are you still my friend? Check _____ yes or _____ no.

Interestingly enough, research suggests that the social success children experience during this time in their childhood significantly impacts their social success throughout their lives. The more success a child has in developing friendships during these very trying years, the more success they will have with friendships throughout their teens and adulthood. Kids seem to be intuitively aware of how very important this is to their future. Unfortunately, many children attempt to avoid this very important and often stressful time by "hiding out" on the internet. Children find safety and comfort in hiding behind their virtual identity. The anonymity of technology based communication allows children to try on a variety of identities, invent for themselves any façade they want, and contemplate responses to others. This allows children the "illusion" of developing social competence, rather than developing real social competence. As difficult as social relating may be for children and teens, it is a challenge they need to master, not avoid.

Empathy Development

The development of empathy is the most important social skill our children can learn. Empathy basically refers to the awareness that an individual gains of other people's feelings, and the impact of their own behavior on others. Children who master this skill are better equipped to deal with life as social creatures. Research suggests children with a well defined sense of empathy get along better with peers, have better relationships with teachers and adults, are more likely to perform well academically and are less likely to get in legal trouble as teens. Empathy is an attachment based skill. It can only be developed within the context of ones' relationships with others. When children see and experience how what they say and do impacts others, they learn to modify their behavior with other people's feelings in mind.

Technology presents some challenges to the development of empathy. When children text, instant message, or communicate through Facebook, Myspace or other social networking sites, they cannot see the impact their words have on others. If they cannot see the impact, they tend to minimize it and become callus to the type of communication in which they are participating. This is one of the reasons why kids tend to say things online they would never say face to face.

Quite simply, the more technological communication replaces face to face communication, the weaker a child's empathy development will be a teen and an adult.

Having a Plan

It is essential today that parents approach technology with a well developed, thought out and confident plan. If parents are not confident in the limits they set for their children, children will sense this, and make it a mission to "wear their parents down." Be prepared for the reality that children will likely respond to any of your limits of their technology by accusing you of being the only parent in the entire universe to have such stupid rules. It is important as the parents of the household, to decide it will be you and not your child, who decides the limits and rules regarding the use of technology in your household. The more prepared parents are, the more confident they will be about what boundaries they set.

The Technologically Savvy Parent

When children begin hiding out in the computer room, communicating with their peers "under the radar," through cell phone conversations, text messaging, and walking around with iPod ear buds in, parents find themselves gradually being "blocked" from their children's lives. Parents then have no idea who their child is speaking to, and no idea what their children are saying or planning. Parents miss out on opportunities to chat with their children's friends. The challenge for parents becomes "How do we integrate technology into our family without losing our attachment to our children, and without losing our ability to responsibly monitor our children's interactions with others.

The following guidelines are designed to help with this challenge.

1. Cell Phones
Children need a gradual introduction to these devices. I strongly urge parents to hold off on purchasing their children their "own" phone until you feel it is absolutely necessary. Despite what we are led to believe through television commercials, our children will not be a social outcast if they do not have a cell phone. In most cases, children do not really need their own phones until they start driving. I realize this seems like a terribly long time to wait for a phone, so I encourage parents to at least wait until ninth grade.

2. Go slowly
Initially, children can "borrow" a phone from the parents. First cell phones need to be used with restrictions, (i.e. to call parents or other limited numbers, and time limits). Children need to be given limits on their minutes and these limits need to be enforced. Very often when kids exceed their limits, parents respond by purchasing plans with unlimited minutes. This does little to help the child learn how to regulate

themselves. I am not an advocate of unlimited anything with children. When children exceed their minutes, which they inevitably do, they need to pay for those minutes and temporarily lose the use of their phones. For example, if they are allotted 300 minutes per month and they use 400, they loose the phone for a third of the following month.

3. House phones!
When your children are home, require them to make and receive calls on the house line, provided you have a land line. My son's friends knew this was the expectation in our home, and they did not hesitate to call our home phone. This allowed me to be aware of who was calling, and gave me an opportunity to stay in touch with my son's friends.

4. Implement Curfews
Cell phones need to be turned off <u>and</u> turned in at a certain time every evening. Kids find it hard to resist the temptation of carrying on conversations in the middle of the night. Even if your child is not "making" any late night calls, the odds are fairly good that they are receiving them.

5. Texting
If teens find it hard to regulate their phone use, they find it almost impossible to limit their texting. Young teens often do not have the maturity to regulate themselves, and it is usually a good idea to not have the texting features as part of the service. As with cell phone minutes, I encourage parents to purchase plans that limit text messaging.

6. Monitoring
Since technology makes monitoring our children more difficult, we have to be savvier, more creative and more diligent. Parents often wonder if diligent monitoring of technology is really necessary. My response is this: "If we

The Technologically Savvy Parent

would not allow our children to spend time in the homes of people we do not know, and we would not allow them to spend time in homes where parents are not present, why would we allow them access to the World Wide Web without our supervision?"

I am a proponent of parents:

➤ *Reviewing cell phone billing to look at what time calls are made and to whom.*

➤ *Checking calling histories and seeing whose numbers your child has stored on his/her phone.*

➤ *Periodically review text messages.*

➤ *Look at the pictures on their digital cameras and phone video cameras.*

➤ *Let your children know you will periodically be taking a look at their Facebook and Myspace sites.*

➤ *Stay on top of computer use by periodically checking the history, blocking certain web sites and being present when your child is instant messaging.*

Parents might want to consider implementing parental monitoring software. There are several programs that provide a range of monitoring. Spector Pro, for example, records a few seconds of computer interaction every few minutes. This gives parents a "sense" of their child's behavior on line without recording every word. Programs such as Web Watcher can be installed and monitored at remote locations. Other programs such as Cyber Sitter, and I Am Big Brother, are also available.

When making a decision about monitoring, parents need to

take several factors into consideration. It is my hope the following discussions of guidelines and monitoring will answer many questions you may have, and assist you in becoming more confident in the decisions you make.

When Screens Should be Introduced

Television and DVD's: Television viewing and movie watching and videos serve no beneficial purpose for children under the age of three. Between conception and three years old, the human brain develops in such a way that it lays the ground work for future development. The brain is a unique organ in that its' development is strongly influenced by its' interaction with its' environment. The infant and toddler brain requires interaction with the people and world that surrounds the child. This interaction does not need to be academic. In fact, it needs to be centered on exploring, playing, physical activity within the child's world; and loving, verbal and physical interaction with adults. Therefore, the less television and video viewing prior to age three, the better.

Video and Computer Games: Recent research confirms what developmental professionals have known for years. Children's play patterns are fairly well established by the age of ten. If video and computer games are introduced at age ten, most children will be able to integrate them into their existing play activity. In other words, they utilize them as an addition to a world rich in leisure activity and are much less likely to use video games obsessively.

When children have the opportunity to spontaneously gather a group of friends together and find ways to entertain themselves with a variety of activities ranging from watching lightening bugs to playing capture the flag, they

The Technologically Savvy Parent

develop a real world sense of competence. The social, physical, emotional, and cognitive skills children learn are immeasurably beneficial.

When my son was young, many people in our neighborhood invested in elaborate backyard play sets. We parents would marvel at the fact that the kids usually ignored the play sets and opted to run around in the woods in our backyards, participating in a variety of activities such as digging holes, creating hills, gathering fallen branches to build log cabins, and playing in the creek. One summer our kids spent an entire week "excavating" the remains of an animal skeleton they found, and piecing it together. This laid the ground work for the life long interest my son has developed for anthropology.

When children have a childhood rich with these types of experiences, video games have a limited appeal. When kids are introduced to video games, the games should become a part of their life experiences, not a substitute for life experiences. I encourage parents to not purchase video or computer games for their children until they are ten; however, don't be concerned if your child chooses to play video games at the homes of their friends. The limited time they have to play these games at the homes of others will be inconsequential.

Cell phones: Part of monitoring children includes monitoring their interaction and communication with peers. Once children have cell phones and begin texting, parents become isolated from their children's communication, creating an inappropriate distance between parent and child. This is an important consideration when deciding when to purchase cell phones for children.

Communication (sometimes intentionally and sometimes unintentionally) goes underground when children start calling one another on their private cell phones, and no longer use the house phone or the parents' cell phones. With elementary and middle school children, parents need to be aware of when their children are communicating and the nature of the communication. The following information may be helpful to parents when deciding when to provide cell phones for their children.

➤ *Elementary age children do not need to have their own cell phones. On the rare occasion when parents feel their children need to have immediate access to them, they can borrow a phone from a family member.*

➤ *Seventh or eighth grade is plenty early for children to have their own phones and waiting until high school is certainly not unreasonable.*

➤ *When preteens or young teens receive their first phone, consider placing limits on the use of the phone. This will help your child learn to later place limits on themselves.*

There are some family plans which limit the numbers which a child can call on their phone. Often, providing phones that only allow the child to make or receive calls from family members is an appropriate way to introduce children to responsible cell phone use. Similarly, parents need to provide clear boundaries when presenting their child with their phones. It is easier to establish boundaries early on, than to try and institute boundaries after problems arise. Boundaries might include limiting the amount of time the children actually have the phone in their possession, and instituting a daily time limit for phone use with friends, imposing family times in which the phone use is off limits

The Technologically Savvy Parent

entirely.

Texting: Adding texting to the technological equation takes parental isolation from their child's social network to an entirely new level. Many parents report that their children sit next to their friends in the back seat of the car and actually text back and forth instead of talking.

Texting has a very powerful appeal to teens because it provides them with an opportunity to think about responses and therefore feel less pressure to come up with a quick response. It also provides them with the ability to control the length, depth and nature of the discussion. It can certainly be a useful tool for teens in broadening their social networks, and expanding their relationships from "school" friends to "out-of-school" friends. Texting can also be a good communication tool for parents and teens. My sons will often text me short bits of interesting information during the day that they would not pick up the phone to share. And with all the technology, texting is appropriate when used as a tool to enhance communication, but not when it is used as a substitute or replacement for other forms of communication.

Unfortunately, texting can present some unique challenges to teens as well as parents. Many teens become obsessive about texting, and have an extremely difficult time limiting their use of texting. Teens also tend to have a difficult time determining the appropriate times for texting. Many teens who would not dream of talking on their phones at the dinner table, or during class, or when involved in a face to face conversation, think nothing of texting during these times. Teens often find themselves texting almost nonstop during class, while watching TV, and doing homework. In my thirty years as a therapist, I have never had to ask teens to refrain from using iPods or cell phones during their sessions; however, I have had to ask teens to not text during their sessions. I am amazed at how difficult it appears to be for teens to resist the temptation to check the text they just received and respond. The instant gratification and the obsessive need to know "what's going on" proves to be irresistible to many teens.

It is easy to understand the appeal texting has for teens. For them, when they constantly text and send pictures to their friends, it feels as if their friends are right there with them to share every experience they encounter during the day. They feel as if their friends are on the shopping trip, at the dinner table, or participating in the family activity. The issue for everyone else in the room is, we didn't invite them.

Sometimes, children and teens need to spend time with family without their friends present. Parents need to be confident in clearly communicating and enforcing boundaries regarding this by reminding kids that there will be no texting during this activity.

Texting also provides teens with opportunities to wander into inappropriate behavior without guidance or accountability from adults. If teens believe that their texts are not going to be monitored by adults, it becomes easy to slip into inappropriate language and inappropriate content while texting. Texting also makes it easy for teens to plan inappropriate activities without the scrutiny of adults. Each week, I hear stories from shocked parents who discover their teens have been sending and receiving sexually explicit text, made arrangements via text messaging to use or purchase drugs, planned deceptive activities, and made arrangements to sneak out of the house in the middle of the night. Certainly teens could make similar plans without the use of text

The Technologically Savvy Parent

messaging; however, texting makes it much easier for teens to plan these activities without detection. After all, I am quite sure that teens do not call one another's house phones late at night to ask their friends if they want to sneak out.

Many teens lack the maturity and moral development to regulate their use of texting or resist the temptation to be drawn into inappropriate behavioral choices, particularly if they feel accountability for these choices unlikely.

Parents can help their children by implementing the following limits:

➤ *Delay adding texting to their children's plans until teens are freshmen or later.*

➤ *Purchase plans that allow parents to limit the times during which texting is allowed. For example, teens do not need texting capacity from 10 PM until 7 AM.*

➤ *Purchase plans that have limited, instead of unlimited texting.*

➤ *Purchase plans that allow parents to monitor via computer, the numbers being texted and the times in which texts are sent and received.*

➤ *Periodically review the texts your children receive.*

➤ *Teach children about appropriate use of texting by requiring they refrain from texting during family times, dinner, homework, or when engaged in conversations with others.*

Facebook and Social Networking Sites

Children push for Facebook accounts at younger and younger ages. It is always wise to remember that what ever you give your child today, they will want more of tomorrow (or perhaps in fifteen minutes). It does not hurt children to wait for things they want. In fact the ability to delay gratification, and work for what one wants is a wonderful asset for kids. My advice to parents is that your child will probably push for Facebook long before you are ready for them to have one. The good news is, you are the parent and you get to decide. I encourage parents to consider the following when making this decision.

➤ Is your child really mature enough to handle the bombardment of social stimuli that comes with Facebook?

➤ Are you ready to relinquish the ability to monitor with whom your child has contact?

➤ Is your child mature enough to regulate themselves and limit their time on Facebook?

➤ Is your child communicative enough that they would share any problems that may surface on Facebook with you?

When considering these questions, most parents would agree that very few middle school children are ready for this

If you say yes to a young teen, the following limits would be appropriate.

➤ Your child will allow you to monitor activity by "friending" you.

➤ Your child understands that inappropriate language or communication will be addressed.

➤ You reserve the right to determine if an individual needs to be "unfriended" based on what you see.

➤ If the child, for any reason, is unable to handle Facebook in a responsible way, the account will be shut down.

If Technology Becomes an Obsession

Technology can and sometimes does become an obsession with children and teens. When technology becomes obsessive, children need parents to step in and assist them by setting limits. As with all behavior, the earlier we intervene, the easier it is to assist the child in changing the behavior.

Early recognition of potential problems is important. The following behaviors are indicators that children are having difficulty regulating their use of technology.

➤ The child appears to be overly focused on some form of technology (very often video games).

➤ The child's social interaction becomes increasingly limited to interaction they have with others through technology.

➤ The child talks about the technology.

➤ The child reduces participation in other activities.

➤ The child lies or covers up the amount of time they spend on technology.

➤ Children place the technological activities in front of other priorities, such as school, chores, friends and family.

➤ Children become angry when something disrupts their access to technology.

➤ When the child is engaged in a technological activity, they block out all other things and are very hard to disengage from the activity.

When parents recognize one or more of these behaviors, it is time to intervene. The first level of intervention is to discuss what you have observed with your child and give them an opportunity to self-correct. Point out specifically what you have noticed. Often children slip into these patterns and are not aware of it.

Encourage the child to come up with a plan that includes negotiating an appropriate amount of time to be spent on technology, when it is appropriate for the child to use technology, and what things need to be taken care of first. Encourage the child or teen to make a list of other things that are more important to them than technology.

If the child is unable to regulate themselves, if they become angry or have emotional outbursts when they are blocked from technology, or if they continue to be dishonest about their use of technology, parents will need to set limits for their children.

Often, parents need to eliminate the use of things, like video games, during the week. In some cases, parents need to eliminate certain forms of technology altogether for awhile. Kids usually become very oppositional when these limits are set. They often make threats as well as promises in order to continue their access to the activity. This is evidence that they need these external controls. Kids often tell me they were initially very angry when their parents limited their games, but they acknowledged they actually feel better once it has been eliminated.

When children become angry and treat their family horribly because they cannot have access to their technology, adults need to help the child step back, evaluate the behavior and regroup.

If you find it necessary to separate your child from the object of their obsession, be prepared to weather the storm. The more resistant they are to discontinuing the obsessive behavior, the more it confirms that you are doing the right thing. If your child substitutes one obsessive behavior for another, it is time to consult a therapist.

The good news is, most children and teens eventually out grow their obsession to things, such as gaming; however, they lose a great deal of very valuable developmental time. This places the child in the position of needing to back track and play catch up on this skill development. Prevention is always easier and less painful than intervention. Setting limits early on and enforcing these limits is helpful to the child and the parents.

Unplug and Tune In

Any discussion of technologically savvy parenting would be incomplete if we did not challenge parents to evaluate their own use of technology. Technology has not only impacted parenting, but it also impacts family dynamics and interaction. In some ways, it has aided in communication and connections with one another. Parents and kids are in verbal contact via cell phones. They often find themselves texting during the day. Some parents and teens find an easy and congenial flow through technology that is perhaps not there during face to face interactions.

In other ways, technology has contributed to the isolation of family members from one another. It is possible for families to be in close physical proximity to one another, and yet to be totally unengaged. A snapshot of the typical American family during any given evening many look something like this: A teenager sits in a corner seat of the family room, texting friends with iPod earphones in. A father is online checking his e-mail. A younger sibling is plopped in the middle of the family room, monopolizing the family television, and engrossed in the most recent video game. Mom is on her cell talking with friends or family. It is so very easy to slip into these patterns without an awareness that it is happening.

In order to insure that family time is not sacrificed to technology time, parents need to be proactive. There are several steps that parents may find helpful.

Implement technology free times. Families benefit from designated family time, when everyone is involved in face to face interaction without technological distractions. Family dinners are a wonderful opportunity for this as long as everyone understands that televisions are turned off and phones do not get answered. Some families enjoy board game nights, bonfires in the back yard, and sitting on the porch chatting. It amazes me how much kids report enjoying these activities.

Share experiences with each other. When my son was a freshman in high school, I pulled into the "circle" at his

The Technologically Savvy Parent

school to wait in line to pick him up and take him home. I watched one day with interest as I noticed that most moms, myself included, had their cell phones attached to their ears. Kids filed out of the building either on phones themselves, or with the iPod earphones plugged in their ears. As kids got in the cars, I noticed that both parents and kids continued their technological activity. At that moment, I realized what opportunities we were missing by being on the phone at a time when we could have spent valuable time with our teens. I made a few changes, the first being that if at all possible, I would not talk on my phone when my son was in the car with me. Second, I asked my son to do the same. Third, I asked my son to share his music by feeding his iPod through the car stereo, or popping in a CD. On long trips, we tend to stay away from movies in the DVD player, and listen to books on CD. The difference is that we are able to share experiences. I learned a great deal about my son's music and his friends are often amazed that I know what he is referring to when he talks about a particular band. He also has a good feel for the type of music I like, and often says, "Mom, listen to this song. I think you'll really like this group."

Share the screens. Sharing the use of the family television, DVD players, house phones and family computers teaches family members to regulate themselves. It also teaches many valuable lessons, such as prioritizing, compromising, and behaving in an emphatic manner because children realize, they're not the only one in the house. It is wise for adults to consider the wisdom and necessity of children having a TV, DVD player, video games and computers in their own rooms. It is time adults ask the questions, "What purpose does this serve?" and "What are the true benefits for the child and the family?"

Set limits on ourself. The best way to teach self

regulating is by role modeling. Limiting ourselves is the best way to teach children to limit themselves.

Talk about the responsible use of technology. Make sure that the children in the family understand socially responsible use of technology. Children need to understand that what they say online does matter and that we expect them to conduct themselves with the same degree of empathy and concern for others online as we would expect of them when talking to others face to face. It amazes me that kids feel free to say things that can be viewed by the entire world that they would not dare whisper to their friends. It is also important to let them know they can come to you if anything ever happens on line that makes them uncomfortable. This includes being bullied or picked on, as well as feeling they are in danger from a possible predator. Parents need to make sure that children understand that even though we have rules we expect to be followed, the most important thing to us is the well being of our children. Therefore, if they do get involved in something they should not have, we are more concerned about them coming to us for help than we are with the fact that they have broken a rule.

CHAPTER FIVE
Confidence, Wit & Wisdom

Quick Tips for Parenting with Confidence, Wit and Wisdom

Parenting with confidence involves keeping ones sense of humor and maintaining a perspective in which common sense takes precedence over fads, myths, anxiety, and other parent's peer pressure. In this final chapter, I will offer a few of my favorite tidbits of wit and wisdom that have served me well as a parent and as a therapist.

1. **Love the child you have because you can't return him or her.** One of the most important things parents can do is see their children with clarity and acceptance. That does not mean passively accepting inappropriate behavior. It does mean learning to accept their basic temperament and personality. Traits and characteristics which emerge early and are displayed consistently, throughout childhood and adolescence, may look different as the child matures; however, they are probably going to always be there. Accept, celebrate, work around or through these personality traits, and understand that the world is made up of, and in fact needs a cast of colorful and unique players. In this culture where it seems we want to medicate all children until they fit into a neat little box of hyper-focused, hyper-achieving, hyper-talented extensions of parental egos—I am sure there is room for your child's unique personality.

2. **Never forget, there are many measures of success.** How many times do parents say, "They will never be successful if they don't _____." (Fill in the blank with parent's pet peeve, such as, get organized, learn to clean their room, quit waiting until the last minute to do their homework, etc.) The truth is that we do need to strive to teach our children these things. It is also true children will

learn to do these things when they start to matter to them. Some children who are slobs grow into very neat and orderly adults. Some children who are slobs grow up and continue to be slobs. Many of the things that drive us crazy have nothing to do with children succeeding as adults. In fact, I have it on good authority that there are successful adults in the world who leave wet towels on the floor. My advice is to address it, but don't let it make you crazy.

3. Very few children actually work up to their potential. One of the most common complaints I hear from parents, teachers and coaches is their children are not working up to their potential. I have to suppress the urge to look at the adults and ask, "Do you?" Because seriously, who really does? In all likelihood, your child will be just fine working somewhere below what we believe to be their potential.

4. Kids should be allowed to do things just because they are fun! We are witnessing a culture of children and teens that are stressed, anxious, and have few skills for dealing with this stress and anxiety. We tend to take things that could be stress-reducing and turn them into things that are stress-producing. Sometimes, kids just want to do things because they are fun. They don't want to practice, get yelled at or lectured, and worry about feeling they are not good enough. In other words, kids want to do things that adults feel are a waste of time. And, they should be allowed to do them. Everything should not be a competition, an achievement, a victory or yet another thing to put on their college application. If they want to ride a skateboard, jump ramps on their bikes, play a musical instrument, hit a golf ball around, they should be allowed to do so without adults stepping in and insisting on lessons, achievements and accomplishments. Developing leisure time activities is one of the best stress and anxiety management tools children can possess. Perhaps we should not only encourage them.

Perhaps we should join them.

5. Grades are not the measure of a child's worth. I understand that we live in a competitive world and parents are terrified that their children will be doomed to a life of misery and unhappiness if their grades are not good. Certainly we should encourage our children to do their best academically, give them any assistance they need to succeed, and hold them accountable to consequences if they do not function in an academically responsible manner. However, we need to keep in mind that many kids are academic late bloomers. Most kids find their motivation. Some find it later than others. Parents often ask me, "What college will this child get into with these grades?" I often respond, "The college where they belong." In other words, children or teens may have to take detours to get where they want to go. It is important to remember that detours are not dead end streets.

Remember, if your child is not doing well at school, school is probably their least favorite thing in the world to talk about. Don't let this become the only thing you discuss with your child. Don't let it be the lens through which you see your child. If school becomes a power struggle, your child will stop doing school work just to prove that you can't make him/her do their school work.

I have known some truly amazing teens that got C's in school. I have known some amazing teens that got A's in school. However, I have also known many unhealthy and dysfunctional teens that made good grades. For some kids the world is their classroom. For some kids, the classroom is their world. Both types of kids have a great deal to offer.

So set your expectations, give them consequences, and then don't say anything else. Don't nag, argue, and yell, because the bottom line is you cannot force your child to do their school work. It's our job to hold them accountable; the rest is up to them. Most importantly, don't allow conflicts over grades to destroy your relationship with your child.

6. You get what you focus on. As parents, we tend to focus on the things we are worried about. I jokingly say the main thing I focused on with my son was his kindness. When his teachers would talk about his struggle in math, I would say, "I know, but is he kind to others?" After all, I am living proof that one can get through life with minimal math skills. So I ended up with a very kind son, who was not so great at math. My bad!

On a more serious note, I think it is natural for parents to over focus on things that frighten or concern them. When parents have big fears, these fears are often rooted in the parents past. In an attempt to prevent what they most fear for their children, parents often over emphasize the thing they fear the most. The overemphasis becomes a self-fulfilling prophecy for the child.

I have known parents who have obsessed about things such as teen pregnancy, academic failures, alcohol and drug problems, or that their child will select the wrong friends or romantic partners. I have also witnessed parents being overly concerned their children might experience psychiatric or emotional problems. While it is appropriate to try and protect our children, warn them about things, and monitor their mental health, it is wise to remember that a little bit goes a long way. I often caution parents that over emphasis on any negative or potential problem almost will guarantee the problem will manifest itself in your family. Over focus does not prevent, in fact it invites it.

7. Your children are not afraid of you and its okay. Parents often report that they are surprised that their children do not seem to fear them. They often say, "I would never have dreamed of doing that to my parents. I would have been scared to death. All my parents had to do was look at me. Why do my kids push me so hard?"

Our kids don't react to us the way we reacted to our parents because our parents did not interact with us the way we interact with our kids. We are a generation of parents who play with our children. We take them fun places. We completely plan our schedules around their entertainment. They are familiar with us. They know how far they can push and exactly what buttons they can push. They know what makes us crazy and what makes us happy. They also know how to call our bluffs.

This is vastly different than what most of us experienced with our own parents. Many of us would readily admit our parents did not play with us; they did not spend their lives in the car hauling us from point A to B. They were not obsessively concerned about our entertainment. Our parents had better things to do than pal around with us. Therefore, many of us would agree we did not grow up being familiar with our parents. There was a sense of mystery around our parents. As a result, we did not push because we were never quite sure what would happen, but we had a sense that whatever it was, it would not be pleasant.

I am not saying one style of parenting is better than the other. I am merely pointing out that they are different. Therefore, parents have to respond in a manner that accounts for this change.

8. Don't forget your goal as you are making your point.

Confident Parenting In A Complex World-

In day to day family life, it is easy to get caught up in the overwhelming schedules, the trivial details of daily life, and frustration over the colorful dynamics of various personalities that exist in one home. In this scenario it is easy to lose sight of the goal we have for our children. Usually, when we get caught up in power struggles, repeated conflicts, arguments and negative communication, it is more about making our point than it is about achieving our goal. It is important to periodically step back, think about the point of our goals, and refocus our energy towards our goals. We may also need to remind ourselves we have a lot of time to reach these goals, there is more than one way to get there, and we are looking for progress, not perfection. This helps keep us centered, responding to day to day issues without over reacting and seeing the positives as our children grow and develop. More importantly, it helps us determine what is a big deal, and what is minor. This in turn, helps teach our children what is most important. Most importantly, it will help remind us that while many things children and teens do may be nerve shatteringly annoying, they are not usually earth shatteringly important.

9. If we allow our children to be the age they are today, tomorrow will take care of itself. Childhood and adolescence is about development. Children go through phases at each age that allow them to learn and grow. Each phase lays the ground work for the developmental tasks that come next. In this culture in which parents are anxious and hyper focused on achievement, we are always getting our kids ready to get ready, instead of just letting them be the age they are now. It is easy for parents to fall into a pattern of experiencing anxiety over every test, every homework assignment and every ball game. We constantly worry and talk about whether our children will be ready for the future. We make kindergarten more difficult to get them ready for first grade. Really? I mean come on, its kindergarten! While I certainly believe we should offer our children every opportunity to blossom, the truth is that children blossom in their very own time frame and their gifts, strengths and talents all surface at different times or in their own unique ways. Let's not be so focused on what we feel they should be doing that we miss out on the celebrating of what they actually are doing. The fact they are growing implies they are learning and they don't know everything yet. And that's okay. Sometimes, in our attempts to prepare children for the next phase of life, adults love to point out how woefully ill-prepared they are. Unfortunately, that tactic does nothing but overwhelm conscientious, hard-working kids, and discourages kids who have a tendency to be a bit more laid back in their approach to life. If we want to help prepare children for the future we can help them do the best they can today, patiently assist them in learning what they are trying to master, let them know what they need to know next (not what they need to know in the distant future) and verbalize our confidence in their ability to figure it all out.

Long term commitments with long term payoffs

Parents are concerned about how to parent with the ever changing culture, its technology and the changes it has created for our children and their worlds. Value based parenting is a tough job. Utilizing discipline in an effective manner can be difficult. Understanding and responding to technology can be challenging. The goal of this book is to provide parents with guidelines to develop a family atmosphere that promotes value development, utilizing

Confident Parenting In A Complex World-

effective discipline that promotes value development, and empowering parents to respond confidently to technology.

In the age of immediate gratification, fax machines, microwaves and drive through windows, it is easy to get caught up in the mania of immediacy. Although we have been able to find time-saving, efficient ways to cut corners in many functions of our daily lives, there are some things that have no quick and easy answers. Parenting children, rearing them to be responsible, healthy contributing adults cannot be done with quick fixes and quick techniques. Healthy adulthood comes from a childhood of events that shape, teach and mature. As parents and as a culture, we must remember that rearing value based children requires us to learn to use value based consequences. We must look beyond the immediate and remember to view our children and our parenting these children, as long-term commitments, long-term obligations, with long-term payoffs.

About the Author...

JANICE GABE, LCSW, CADAC is the president and founder of <u>New Perspectives of Indiana</u>, a therapy, training, and consultation corporation in Indianapolis, Indiana. Janice has dedicated her entire professional career to working with children, teens and families. Janice has over thirty years of clinical experience and prides herself on providing nurturing, effective, innovative and cutting edge treatment to each and every client that she sees.

Janice is a sought after speaker and has provided workshops and trainings to parents, teens, educators and treatment professionals around the country. She has consulted with numerous schools, communities, mental health centers and addictions treatment facilities to assist them in developing programs for teens and families. Janice is recognized as one of the country's leading experts on the needs and issues facing children and families.

Most important to Janice, she and her husband are the lucky parents of two amazing sons.

The material by
Janice Gabe
on the following page
is available for purchase.

Call, fax or send your order to:

Professional Resource Publications
P.O. Box 501485
Indianapolis, IN 46256
(317) 465-9688 • (317) 465-9689 (FAX)

* Indiana Residents also include a 6% sales tax.
** A 20% restock fee may be charged for any returns.

ORDER FORM

(Tear off page or copy both sides on printer to mail in order)

VIDEO TAPES:
_____ "Is it Adolescence or Pathology?"
($50 each tape;
$5.95 S&H for 1, $3 each additional tape)

"Cultures of Change"
_____ Tape 1 – "Parenting in Cultures of Change"
_____ Tape 2 – "Value Based Parenting"
_____ Tape 3 – "Value Based Discipline"
($50 each tape; $5.95 S&H for 1, $9.95 for all 3)

DVD VIDEOS:
_____ "Beyond Diagnosis: The ADHD Child"
_____ "Kids and Pot: A Word About Weed"
($100 each video; $3 S&H each)

AUDIO TAPES:
_____ "Celebrating The Kindergarten Child"
_____ "Parenting in Cultures of Change"
($7 each tape; S&H $0.75 cents each)

BOOKS:
_____ "A Professional Guide to Dual Diagnosis Disorders"
($17.00 each; $3 S&H for 1, $0.75 each additional book)

_____ "Making the Grade: The Teen's Guide to Homework Success"
($7.95 each; $3 S&H for 1, $0.75 for each additional)

"Adolescent Co-occurring Disorders Workbooks"
_____ "Substance Use and Mood Disorders
_____ "Substance Use and Anxiety Disorders"
($55 each workbook;
$5.95 S&H for 1, $2 for each additional)

~ TOTALS & INFORMATION ON THE BACK OF THIS PAGE ~

Sub Total $_____

Indiana residents only, add 6% sales tax $_____

Shipping $_____

Total $_____

SHIPPING AND PAYMENT INFORMATION:

NAME: _____

ADDRESS: _____

_____

DAY PHONE: _____ CELL PHONE: _____

CHECK ENCLOSED: _____ OR CREDIT CARD INFO: _____

VISA _____ MASTERCARD _____ AMERICAN EXPRESS _____

CARD NUMBER: _____

EXPIRATION DATE: _____

SIGNATURE: _____